Reader's Digest Needlecraft Guides

CANVAS WORK

Reader's Digest Needlecraft Guides

CANVAS WORK

Step-by-step instructions for over 75 stitches

Published by The Reader's Digest Association Limited
LONDON ● NEW YORK ● SYDNEY ● CAPETOWN ● MONTREAL

READER'S DIGEST NEEDLECRAFT GUIDE: CANVAS WORK
First published 1995
Copyright © Text and Illustrations 1995, 1981

The material in this book first appeared in
READER'S DIGEST COMPLETE GUIDE TO NEEDLEWORK
First edition Copyright © 1981
Reprinted 1991
The Reader's Digest Association Limited,
Berkeley Square House, Berkeley Square, London W1X 6AB

Copyright © 1981 Reader's Digest Association Far East Limited
Philippines Copyright 1981 Reader's Digest Association Far East Ltd

Printed in Italy

ISBN 0 2764 2181 7

CONTRIBUTORS

The publishers would like to thank the following people for major contributions to this series.

Consultant editor Eirian Short

Editorial contributors and designers

Louise Amble   Peggy Bendel   Sherry De Leon   Rosemary Drysdale   Katherine Enzmann   Phoebe Fox   Zuelia Ann Hurt
Barbara H. Jacksier   Joyce D. Lee   Susanna E. Lewis   Claudia Librett   Victoria Mileti   Edna Adam Walker
Monna Weinman   Joanne Whitwell

Technical assistance

Elspeth Arnold   Lesley Arnold   Betty Beeby   Linda Blyer   Barbara Dawson   Janet Eaton   Charlotte Feng-Veshi
Sheila Gore   Jane Iles   Diana Keay   Elizabeth Kerr   Arlene Mintzer   Carole Nolan   Erwin Rowland
Cathie Strunz   Valentina Watson   Joan Webb

Contributing artists

Roberta W. Frauwirth   Susan Frye   Pat Kemmish   John A. Lind Corp.   Marilyn MacGregor   Mary Ruth Roby   Jim Silks
Randall Lieu   Ray Skibinski   Lynn E. Yost

Contributing photographers

J. D. Barnell   Bruton Photography   Joel Elkins   Ken Korsh   Ross McCann/Conrad-Dell-McCrann, Inc.   Michael A. Vaccaro

Research assistance

Aero Needles (Abel Morrall)   Appletons Bros Ltd   C. J. Bates & Son   Emile Bernat & Sons Co.   Bernina Sewing Machines
Boye Needle Company   Brunswick Worsted Mills Inc.   J. & P. Coats   Cowling & Wilcox   Craftsman's Mark
The D.M.C. Corporation   Embroiderers' Guild   Frederick J. Fawcett Inc.   T. Forsell & Son   Harrods Ltd
Harry M. Fraser Company   Hayfield Textiles   Hosiery Machine Co.   Kreinik Mfg Co.   Lowe & Carr   H. Milward & Sons
Newey Goodman   Paternayan Bros Inc.   Paton & Baldwins   Phildar International   Pingouin   Reynolds Yarn Inc.
Royal School of Needlework   Singer Company (UK) Ltd   Sirdar   Talon/Donahue Sales Div. of Textron   Joan Toggitt Ltd
Twilleys of Stamford   Vilene   Whitecroft Scovill   Wm. E. Wright Co.

Cover

Photography by Paul Biddle   Craftwork supplied by Dora Lockyer

Canvas work

'Fleurs de mon pays', designed by Shirley Brickendon for Montreal Museum of Fine Arts.

Canvas work basics

What canvas work is

Canvas work is the technique of forming stitches on a special open-weave fabric known as canvas. Canvas is constructed of *vertical* and *horizontal* threads that are woven together to produce precisely spaced *holes* between threads. The points at which these threads intersect are known as *meshes*. All canvas work stitches are worked to make use of the grid-like structure of the canvas.

Basically, any canvas work stitch can go in only two directions, either diagonally across or parallel to the canvas threads and meshes (see the stitch direction sample below). The direction the thread takes is dictated by the kind of stitch that is being worked. Several canvas work stitches fall in only one direction; others require threads to be laid in several directions or even to be crossed over each other.

The size of a stitch depends upon two things. One of these is the character of

the stitch. Certain of the stitches span only one canvas thread or mesh; other stitches span two or more. Stitch size also depends on the gauge of canvas that the stitch is being worked on. (The gauge of a canvas is the number of meshes to each 2.5 cm of that canvas.) The more meshes per 2.5 cm a canvas has, the smaller the stitches worked on it can be. Canvas is available in many gauges (see p. 8); this wide overall range breaks down into two subgroups, **petitpoint** and **grospoint**. A petitpoint canvas is one with 16 or more meshes; a grospoint canvas has fewer than 16 meshes. Because a petitpoint canvas has more meshes per centimetre than a grospoint canvas, any stitch worked on a canvas in the petitpoint range will be smaller than it would be on a grospoint canvas. Petitpoint and grospoint stitching are shown actual size in the two samples below, right. The same stitch,

tent stitch, is used in both, and the area of canvas is also the same. The first sample is done on a 24-gauge canvas, which is well within the petitpoint range of canvases; the second sample is on a 12-gauge canvas, which falls in the grospoint range.

Stitch size affects the amount of working time and the durability of the finished item. In general, the smaller the stitches, the more time will be spent in working them and the more durable the finished item will be. More time is required for small stitches, of course, because it takes more of them to cover the canvas. Small stitches are more durable than large ones because they are less likely to be snagged or broken when the finished canvas work is in use. How hardwearing an item needs to be depends on its end use. A cushion, for example, will be subject to more hard wear than a wall hanging.

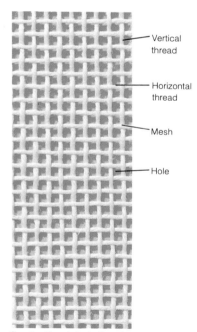

Construction of single thread canvas

Directions stitches can take on canvas

Petitpoint stitches

Grospoint stitches

The three types of canvas work

The interpretation of the overall drawn design on which a finished canvas work is based depends upon the stitches. They can affect a design in two ways. First, the stitches can alter the drawn lines of the design. Differences between drawn and stitched lines occur because the stitches must be worked to conform to the grid-like structure of the canvas. Drawn lines, of course, are free of such restrictions. How much deviation there is between the two lines depends on the character of the stitch and its size. The other way the stitch can affect a design arises from the texture or pattern the stitching produces. Interpretation in texture changes design elements drastically, greatly altering the design's visual impact. Canvas work offers a wide choice of texture possibilities. For illustrations and explanations of a comprehensive assortment of canvas work stitches and the many textures and patterns they produce, see pp. 12–55.

When you are deciding which stitches to use, bear in mind that three distinct visual impressions can be produced by means of canvas work stitches (see the three stitched samples below). The first sample illustrates the effect of **tent stitches** on a design. Tent stitch is a small diagonal stitch that spans only a single canvas mesh. Though there are different ways of working tent stitches, each method produces the same stitch and even texture on the right side of the canvas. Because tent stitches are small, they can interpret a drawn line fairly precisely; the smaller the stitches, the truer the stitched line will be to the drawn line. A design to be executed in tent stitches, therefore, can be fairly detailed and include varying degrees of subtle shading.

All other stitches could be categorised as **ornamental stitches.** This group embraces many stitches, each varying in size, texture and pattern. A design intended for ornamental stitches tends to be less detailed than one meant for tent stitches, usually relying on the structural elements of a design rather than on its details. There are two reasons for this. First, virtually all ornamental stitches are large, and so less suited to following drawn lines. Second, the textures produced by ornamental stitches interpret and enhance the physical reality of design elements exceptionally well. The second sample below follows the same basic design used for the tent stitch sample next to it. Notice how much more prominent than design details major elements have become, and how well the knotted stitch (see p. 39) suggests the texture of wood for the barn, the diamond eyelet (p. 47) the window of the barn, the leaf stitch (see p. 48) the tree. Stitch selection, however, is just

one factor to consider when composing a design that will be carried out in canvas work. For a more thorough explanation of designing, see pp. 56–57.

Included in the ornamental stitch classification are the **Florentine stitches** that produce the third type of canvas work. Florentine stitches are straight canvas work stitches placed parallel to the threads of the canvas. Many patterns can be produced with Florentine stitches, but one of the most familiar and classic is the chevron design (see third sample below). Florentine stitch is based on the customary straight stitches, but they are placed in a zigzag line across the canvas. With many Florentine embroideries, the overall finished design is determined by the structure of the stitch rather than the selection of a stitch to fill in a predetermined shape. For more details on Florentine work, see p. 67.

Design done in tent stitches

Same design worked in ornamental stitches

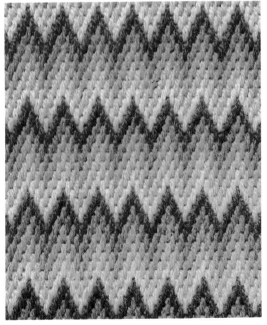

Arrangement of Florentine stitches

7

Canvas work basics/Tools and materials

Canvases

Canvas is fundamental to the success of any canvas work project, and so should be selected with the utmost care. Be sure the threads are free of knots and cuts. Most canvases are made of cotton or linen. Some newer ones are made of synthetic fibres; some fine-gauge canvases come in silk. The gauge should be suitable for the item and design being worked (see pp. 56–57).

To determine the gauge of a canvas, hold a ruler along a horizontal thread and count the meshes in 2.5 cm. In the photograph above, this is being done on a 10-gauge single canvas.

There are several different types of canvas. Those used most often are plain single, interlock single, and double. Both **plain and interlock single** canvases have a single-mesh structure; the construction of the mesh, however, is different in each. A single mesh of the plain canvas is formed by the intersection of a single vertical and a single horizontal thread. With interlock canvas, each vertical thread is actually two thinner threads that have been twisted around each other and a single horizontal thread to produce a 'locked' single mesh. The locked construction of the interlock canvas is more stable than the merely intersecting mesh of plain canvas. All canvas work stitches can be formed successfully on an interlock canvas; plain single canvas, however, is not suitable for use with certain canvas work stitches, such as the half-cross stitch (see p. 14). Both the plain and interlock canvases are available in a wide range of gauges.

Double canvas (sometimes known as Penelope) has a double-mesh construction. The double mesh is formed by the intersection of pairs of vertical threads with pairs of horizontal threads. Besides being strong, a double mesh has a second advantage – it can be adjusted so that stitches of different sizes can be worked on the same piece of canvas (see photograph below). Used as is, a double

mesh can accept one size of stitch; when the pairs of threads are separated, four plain meshes are formed that are capable of receiving four smaller stitches. The double-mesh adaptability is advan-

tageous when your design calls for finely stitched areas. The gauge of a double canvas is given as two numbers separated by a line, for example, 10/20. The smaller number designates the number of double meshes per 2.5 cm; the larger number, the meshes per 2.5 cm if threads are separated. Double canvas is readily available in 5/10 to 14/28 gauges.

In another type, **rug canvas**, each mesh is formed by two vertical threads that are twisted around each other and a pair of horizontal threads. Threads cannot be separated. Rug canvas comes in 3 to 5 gauges, and is used primarily for rugs.

Canvas may be bought with the design printed or painted on in full colour. Subjects range from abstract patterns to naturalistic pictorial scenes.

Plastic canvas is moulded rather than woven into a stiff, medium-gauge canvas-like form. Sold in cut pieces in kits used for items such as rugs.

Plain single canvas

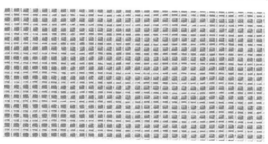

Double canvas

Printed canvas

Interlock canvas

Rug canvas

Synthetic canvas

Threads

Threads for canvas work come in several fibres, weights and textures, as well as many lovely colours. Shown below are the types of threads most often used. The weight of thread varies with the type: tapestry wool, for example, is thinner than rug wool. The thread should be thin enough to slide through the holes of the canvas easily and without distortion, but thick enough to cover the canvas in stitch form. In general, the larger the canvas gauge, the heavier or thicker the thread should be. Appropriate thread weight depends also on the stitch that is being formed (p. 12).

Strand and *ply* are two terms relating to thread structure that need to be understood. A strand is the unit; a ply is a part of a strand. For example, Persian wool is made up of three strands of wool, but each of these strands consists of two plies. Strands are easily separated, which allows you to decrease or increase the number of strands as necessary to produce wool of a particular thickness. Plies are not easily separated. Canvas work threads are made of several different fibres, such as wool, cotton, silk, rayon and metallic threads. Wool is used most often. This is because it is an inherently strong fibre that has proved very durable for canvas work.

A thread selected for use in canvas work should have the capacity to withstand abrasion both while the stitch is being worked and when the finished item is in use. If the canvas work item will not get hard use, less sturdy fibres, such as rayon and metallic, can be used.

Another strength factor is the length of the fibres used in manufacturing the thread. The fibres in canvas work wools are longer, and therefore stronger, than those that are used in the wools made especially for knitting. This is why knitting wools are not recommended as substitutes for canvas work wools.

Needles

The needle type recommended for use in canvas work is the tapestry needle. It has a large eye that allows for easy threading, and a blunt point that prevents the needle from piercing the canvas threads. Tapestry needles are available in a range of sizes from 14, the heaviest, to 26, the finest. The finer the size, the shorter the needle and the smaller its eye. Select the needle size according to the gauge of the canvas that is being worked. The needle should be thin enough to be passed easily through the holes of the canvas without distorting them. The 18 needle is used most often, since it is suitable for the popular 10 and 12-gauge canvases. Needles from 20 to 26 are used on the finer-gauge canvases; those from 13 to 16, on heavier canvases. Test any needle to make sure it is the correct size. Tapestry needles are usually sold in packages of several needles; they may be one size only or an assortment of sizes.

Persian wool. A 2-ply, 3-strand wool. Strands of this wool can be used singly or in multiples, depending on the thickness required for the canvas and stitch. Because of this adaptability in weight, Persian wool is a versatile canvas work thread.

Tapestry wool. A 4-ply, single-strand wool, slightly finer than three strands of Persian wool. Plies are difficult to separate.

Rug yarn. A very thick 3-ply, single-strand thread that is most often used for rugs. Comes in wool, acrylic, and a rayon/cotton blend. Thickness of the thread varies with the fibre content.

Crewel wool. A fine 2-ply, single-strand wool most often employed in crewel embroidery. It is slightly finer than one strand of Persian wool.

Stranded cotton. A multiple-strand thread which can be separated easily to produce differing thicknesses. There are also stranded silk and rayon threads.

Pearl cotton. A 2-ply, single-strand thread made in three different thicknesses: 3 (heavy), 5 (medium) and 8 (fine). Made of cotton only, has a slight sheen. The 5 is about the same thickness as crewel wool.

Soft embroidery cotton. A 5-ply, single-strand thread that is soft and has a dull finish.

Metallic thread. Available in various weights, textures and colours (besides silver and gold). Not very durable; used for small areas.

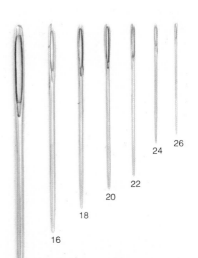

Tapestry needles have large eyes and blunt points, making them the perfect needle for all canvas work. They range in size from 14, the heaviest, to 26, the finest.

14 16 18 20 22 24 26

Canvas work basics/Tools and materials

Frames and holders

In working canvas work, use of a frame or some other kind of canvas holder can be a great help. Such devices help to keep canvas neat and to allow the stitches to be properly laid on to the canvas. They also prevent the canvas from being severely distorted by the stitches. The best device to use is a slate frame; a frame attached to a stand will free both your hands for stitching. Several varieties are shown below. Most canvas work frames work on the same principle. The top and bottom edges of the canvas are first sewn to tapes on rods. Then the canvas is rolled on to the rods and the rods are fastened to the side arms of the frame. The canvas can be narrower but not wider than the tapes. In length, the canvas should not be too much shorter than the side arms; it can be longer, however, since excess length can be rolled on to the rods.

Another device that can serve as a frame is a canvas stretcher. It must be large enough to accommodate the entire piece of canvas. Once the canvas is fixed in place, it should not be re-positioned.

A hoop is best reserved for finer-gauge, softer canvases, which are less likely to be creased by the pressure of the rings.

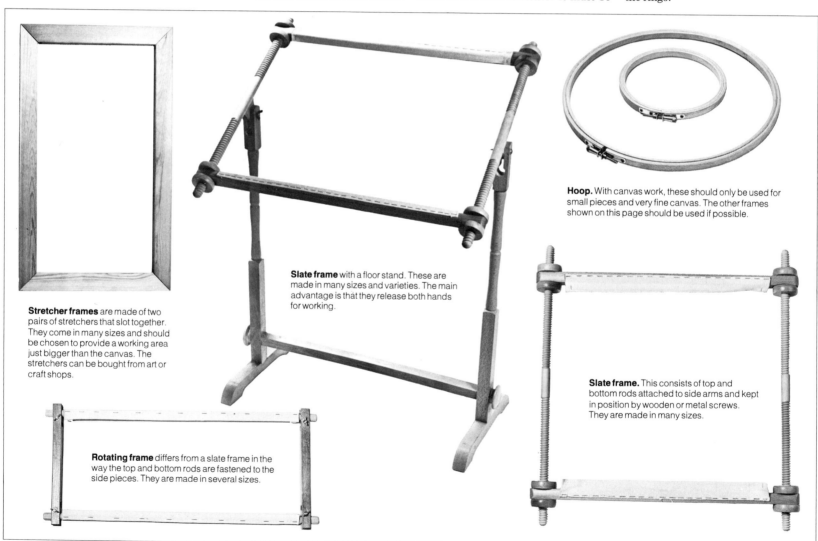

Stretcher frames are made of two pairs of stretchers that slot together. They come in many sizes and should be chosen to provide a working area just bigger than the canvas. The stretchers can be bought from art or craft shops.

Slate frame with a floor stand. These are made in many sizes and varieties. The main advantage is that they release both hands for working.

Rotating frame differs from a slate frame in the way the top and bottom rods are fastened to the side pieces. They are made in several sizes.

Hoop. With canvas work, these should only be used for small pieces and very fine canvas. The other frames shown on this page should be used if possible.

Slate frame. This consists of top and bottom rods attached to side arms and kept in position by wooden or metal screws. They are made in many sizes.

Design transfer needs

If you intend to design your own canvas work, certain tools will be essential, others will make the job easier and more professional. The most necessary tools, of course, are the papers and pens. If you are copying a design from a book, tracing paper is helpful. Graph paper is needed for charting a design; see-through graph paper, for tracing a chart or design. When a design is being coloured on paper, the pen need not be waterproof; it must be, however, when you want to colour a design on canvas. To paint on canvas, choose acrylic paints, thinned with water. When dry, acrylic paints are permanent.

Miscellaneous equipment

Shown below are some pieces of equipment that you will find yourself needing or wanting at different points in the canvas work process. Some you may already have, others you may have to buy. The blocking board and indicator pins will be necessary for stretching the stitched canvas work back into its original shape. The large scissors are for cutting the canvas, the embroidery scissors for cutting threads. Masking tape is ideal for binding canvas edges. A needle threader will make it easier to thread wools; a magnifier will help you do a better job with fine details. A tape measure will be useful.

Graph paper. Available as opaque or transparent paper in centimetre squares.

Tracing paper is sold in many sizes and usually in pads or rolls. It is used to trace designs from drawings or other sources.

Felt-tipped markers are available with fine or broad tips. Waterproof markers should be used.

Paints and brushes are needed if you paint a design on canvas. Acrylic paints are waterproof when dry.

T-square. This is a ruler with a head at right-angles to the body. It is used for drawing grids by sliding the head along the side of a drawing board.

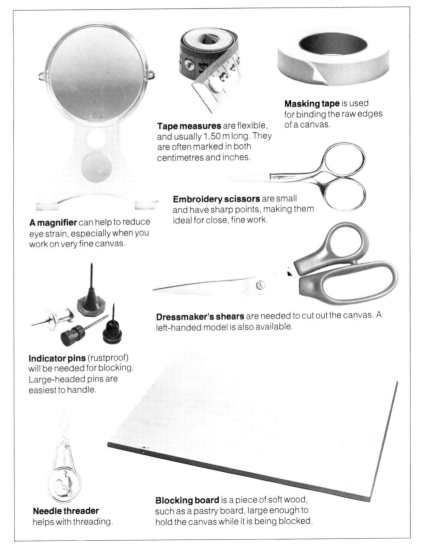

Tape measures are flexible, and usually 1.50 m long. They are often marked in both centimetres and inches.

Masking tape is used for binding the raw edges of a canvas.

A magnifier can help to reduce eye strain, especially when you work on very fine canvas.

Embroidery scissors are small and have sharp points, making them ideal for close, fine work.

Indicator pins (rustproof) will be needed for blocking. Large-headed pins are easiest to handle.

Dressmaker's shears are needed to cut out the canvas. A left-handed model is also available.

Needle threader helps with threading.

Blocking board is a piece of soft wood, such as a pastry board, large enough to hold the canvas while it is being blocked.

Canvas work stitches

General information

The most familiar canvas work stitch is the small, slanted stitch known as tent stitch (see first sample below). It is also the most basic stitch, and one that every embroiderer should master and use. There are many other canvas work stitches, each with its own application. A working knowledge of a variety of stitches can add greatly to the scope and originality of your canvas work projects.

You will find a great many stitches illustrated and explained in the 40-page section that follows. For ease in learning, they have been grouped according to the direction that the thread takes while the stitch is being worked. There are five stitch groups: **diagonal**, **straight**, **crossing**, **composite** and **pile**. An actual-size sample of each stitch accompanies a detailed step-by-step explanation of how that stitch is worked.

The best way to learn the stitches, however, is to do them. Working the stitches yourself will show you, too, which ones can be worked quickly and how much thread is taken up by each. Also, of course, this will give you your own stitch samples. Do this stitching in sampler form, and it will be a permanent and handy reference to help in selecting stitches for a particular project. On p. 56 you will find additional tips on choosing stitches for the enhancement of a particular design. If you decide to make your own sampler, a 10-gauge interlock single canvas and Persian wool will be suitable for most of the stitches. There are only a few, as you will see, that should be done on double canvas. Wool thickness will depend on the stitch that is being done. A discussion of proper stitch tension and thread weight appears on the immediate right; general stitching techniques are explained on the facing page.

The stitches contained in this section are geared to right-handed people. For guidance on how to work if you are left-handed, turn to p. 55.

Stitch tension and thread coverage

As you work canvas work stitches, two things must be observed simultaneously: maintenance of a correct stitch tension and use of a weight of thread that satisfactorily covers the canvas. A good stitch tension allows the thread to be held tautly around the threads of the canvas; when the correct tension is maintained, all the stitches will be formed evenly. Tension that is too loose causes the thread to stand out more than it should from the surface of the canvas. This affects the durability of the stitch; loose threads are susceptible to snagging when canvas work is in use. Tension that is too tight will distort the canvas threads, and stretch the thread too thin as well. If thread is too thin, the canvas will not be well covered. This result is illustrated by the second sample of tent stitches below. In general, the larger the gauge and the longer the stitch, the heavier the thread should be. To combine different stitch sizes successfully on the same piece of canvas, you will most likely have to use different weights of thread. All of the stitches shown below were done on a 10-gauge, interlock single canvas. The first two samples are of tent stitches, both worked with two strands of Persian wool. Coverage is good in the first sample because the stitch tension was correct. In the second tent stitch sample, tension was too tight. The adjoining samples (below right) are of straight Gobelin stitches. Both were worked with the proper tension, but the two strands of Persian wool used in the second sample were too thin for adequate coverage. The first sample was worked with four strands, which, as the result shows, is the proper weight of yarn for the stitch and canvas. Always experiment before beginning a design.

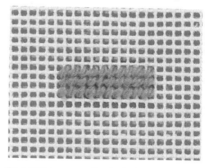

Tent stitches, proper tension/weight

Straight Gobelin, proper tension/weight

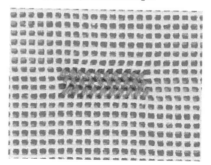

Tent stitches with too-tight tension

Straight Gobelin with too-thin thread

General stitching techniques

There are a few working techniques common to all canvas work stitches. The most basic of these are separating strands of thread and threading a needle; these are explained fully in the Embroidery chapter. Before threading the needle for any canvas work stitch, cut the thread to a 50 cm length. A thread longer than that tends to become frayed as the stitches are being worked. The number of strands will depend on stitch and canvas (see facing page).

In canvas work, there are special methods for securing thread ends. When starting, allow 3 to 5 cm of thread to remain at the back of the canvas. Hold this thread end against the canvas and catch it with the first few stitches. When the end is secured, clip off the excess and continue to work the rest of the stitches. To end a thread, bring needle and thread to the back of the canvas; weave the thread through the underside of the last few stitches, then clip it. Avoid starting and ending threads in line with each other. Instead, stagger their positions; this will avoid the formation of a ridge on the right side of the canvas.

What makes each canvas work stitch different from the other is the way the thread is laid on to the mesh of the canvas. In order for the thread to be properly laid, the canvas must be held correctly while the stitch is worked. Most of the canvas stitches are worked with the canvas held so that the lengthwise threads lie vertically, and a horizontal thread marks the top edge of the canvas. The technique for some stitches requires the canvas to be turned while you are working. With several of the stitches, among them tent stitch (as shown on p. 15), the canvas is turned around for each new row. When these are finished, however, all the stitches lie in the same direction. Sometimes the canvas is given only a quarter-turn. This may be done to produce a particular textural effect (see p. 57), but quite often the quarter-turn simply makes it easier to work a particular stitch. Examples are those stitches, like triangle stitch (see p. 49), in which the thread is laid in four directions.

Almost all of the stitches included in this section are shown worked on single canvas. It should not be assumed from this, however, that a stitch cannot be done on another type of canvas. Where it is necessary to use a particular canvas, this requirement is pointed out. The illustrations also show the stitches being formed by the sewing method, in which the point of the needle is inserted and brought out in a single scooping movement. There is another method, the stabbing method, that involves two separate motions for each stitch. The stabbing method is recommended when the canvas is on a frame; it is difficult to scoop under the canvas threads when a canvas is stretched taut. Both of these methods of forming the stitches are shown below.

With either working method, there is a possibility that the thread may become too twisted. Excessive twist causes thread to kink and knot and to appear thinner than it would in its normal, relaxed state.

To untwist the thread, discontinue stitching and allow the needle and thread to dangle freely. When the thread has unwound itself, resume stitching.

SECURING THREAD ENDS

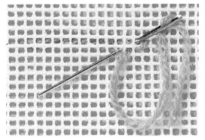

When starting, leave 3 to 5 cm of thread at the back of the canvas. Catch the thread end with the first few stitches; then trim off the excess.

When ending, bring the needle and thread to the back of the canvas. Weave the thread through the backs of the last few stitches; then cut it short.

HOLDING CANVAS WHILE WORKING

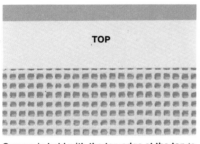

Canvas is held with the top edge at the top to work most canvas stitches. Before beginning, label the top edge of the canvas.

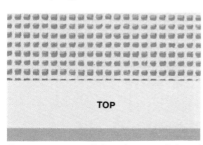

For some canvas stitches, the canvas is turned while you are working. With tent stitch (p. 15), turn canvas for each new row.

METHODS OF STITCH FORMATION

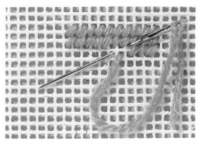

With the sewing method of stitch formation, the needle, in one motion, scoops in for the end of one stitch and out for the start of the next.

The needle is then pulled through the canvas and the thread of the last stitch is positioned over the proper canvas thread or meshes.

The stabbing method requires two movements for each stitch. First, needle and thread are pulled through to right side of the canvas.

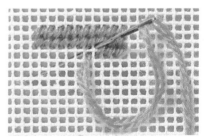

Then the needle and thread are pulled through to the back side of the canvas. The thread of the stitch is laid with the second motion.

Canvas work stitches

Diagonal stitches

The canvas work stitches in this first group are classified as diagonal stitches because all of them are worked to slant diagonally across the threads of the canvas. Included in the diagonal group are the tent stitches, the most familiar and frequently used of all canvas work stitches. Tent stitches produce an even texture applicable to any type of design. They are often used to produce the subtle effect of shading in a flower petal by using several tones of one colour. Each of the other diagonal stitches has its own distinctive texture or pattern. Whether you use any diagonal stitch will depend, first, on whether you find it appealing, and second, on how well its size and pattern meet the requirements of your canvas work design.

Diagonal stitches over one mesh can be formed with either a half-cross or a tent stitch. Tent stitch, which can be worked horizontally, vertically or diagonally, is more hard-wearing than half-cross, but uses up more thread. The diagonal method is often preferred because it distorts the canvas less. Half-cross stitch is difficult to work on single canvas, as the stitches slip at the mesh points. Half-cross can be made more durable by working over a laid thread.

Half-cross stitch (front and back views)

Tent stitch (horizontal, front and back views)

Tent stitch (diagonal, front and back views)

Half-cross stitch (done horizontally). Starting at the upper left, work each row of stitches from left to right. Form each stitch by bringing needle out at 1, then in at 2. At the end of each row of stitches, finish the last stitch and leave the needle at the back of the canvas. Then turn canvas completely around and form the new row in line with the stitches just completed.

CANVAS TURNED

Half-cross stitch (done vertically). Begin at the lower right and work each row of stitches up the canvas. For each stitch, bring needle out at 1, then in at 2. At the end of each row, finish the last stitch and leave needle at back of canvas. Turn the canvas all the way around and form the new row of stitches next to those just done.

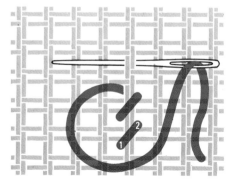
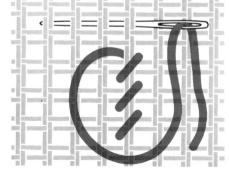

CANVAS TURNED

Tent stitch (done horizontally). Start at upper right and work each row of stitches from right to left. Form each stitch by bringing needle out at 1, then in at 2. At the end of each row of stitches, finish the last stitch and leave needle at back of canvas. Then turn the canvas completely around and work stitches of the new row directly in line with those in the row just completed.

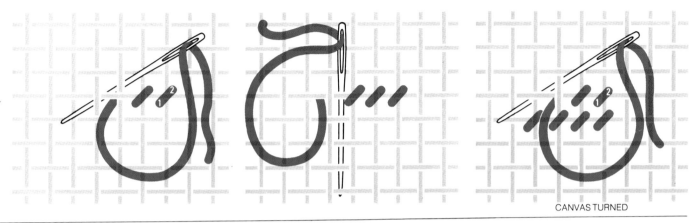

CANVAS TURNED

Tent stitch (done vertically). Start at the upper right and work each row of stitches down the canvas. To form each stitch, bring the needle out at 1, then in at 2. At each row's end, finish the last stitch and leave needle at back of canvas. Then turn the canvas completely around and form new row of stitches next to the row just completed.

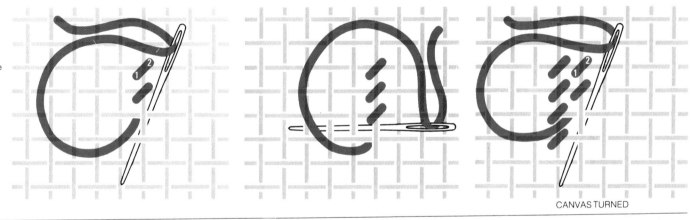

CANVAS TURNED

Tent stitch (done diagonally). Begin a few meshes from upper right and work rows alternately down, then up the canvas. For each stitch, bring needle out at 1, in at 2. Place stitches next to each other in a diagonal row; miss one canvas hole between. To work down, hold needle vertically to go from stitch to stitch. Below last stitch of a down row, form first stitch of an up row. To work up, hold needle horizontally between stitches. Form first stitch of down row next to last stitch of up row. Turn canvas to fill in corner above first row.

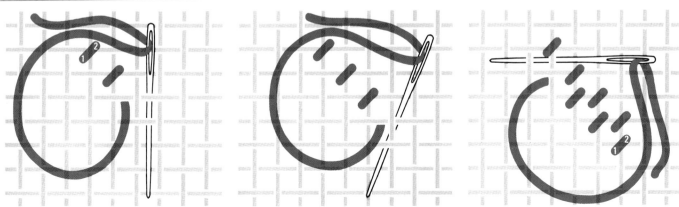

15

Canvas work stitches

Diagonal stitches

Slanted Gobelin stitch

Encroaching slanted Gobelin stitch

SLANTED GOBELIN STITCHES

Each of the individual slanted Gobelin and encroaching slanted Gobelin stitches is formed in the same way; each can vary in size to the same degree. The visual difference between the two is caused by the way the rows of stitches are placed. The rows of slanted Gobelin stitches are kept separate, producing a definite, row-by-row configuration. Rows of encroaching slanted Gobelin stitches overlap, resulting in a single, uniform texture. Both stitches can be adapted in size to suit confined or background areas of a canvas work design.

Slanted Gobelin stitch. Start at upper right and work rows alternately right to left, then left to right. For each stitch, bring needle out at 1, pass it up over canvas, down into 2. Space between 1 and 2 can be from two to five horizontal canvas threads by one to two vertical threads. Spacing here is two horizontal by one vertical thread. At the end of each row, reverse working direction; place new stitches so their bases (1) are one stitch length below bases of stitches in preceding row.

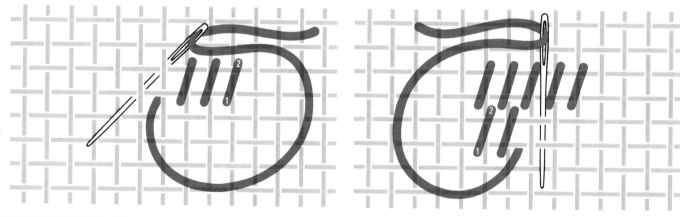

Encroaching slanted Gobelin stitch. Starting at upper right, work rows alternately right to left, then left to right. For each stitch, bring needle out at 1, up over canvas, and down into 2. Space between 1 and 2 can vary as for slanted Gobelin stitches. Space shown here is three horizontal by one vertical canvas thread. At end of each row, reverse the working direction. Position tops (2) of new stitches one canvas hole above and to the right of the bases of the stitches in the preceding row.

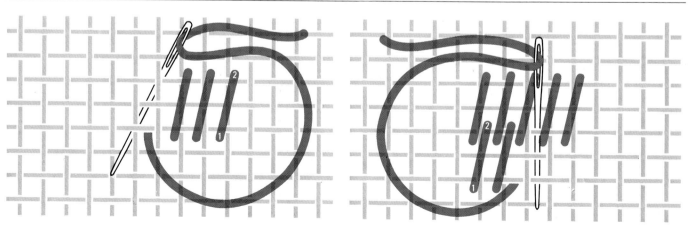

Byzantine stitch

Jacquard stitch

BYZANTINE STITCHES

Byzantine stitch and its variation, jacquard stitch, form striking patterns of diagonal, uniformly stepped rows of stitches. Each stitch in the Byzantine pattern is long and slanted; the jacquard pattern alternates rows of Byzantine stitches with rows of horizontal and vertical tent stitches. The size of both the long stitches and the steps can vary (see below). Both patterns are ideal for use as background in canvas work. A second colour can easily be introduced into either pattern by alternating the colour of thread used for the rows.

Byzantine stitch. Start at upper left corner, work first row, in steps, diagonally down the canvas. Each row is a repetition of six or eight stitches (six here). Half are placed next to each other horizontally, the other half vertically, to form the steps. Form stitches consistently over two to four canvas meshes (two used here, 1 to 2). Subsequent rows are worked alternately up, then down the canvas to first fill in upper, then lower areas. Fit the steps of a new row into steps of preceding row (far right illustration).

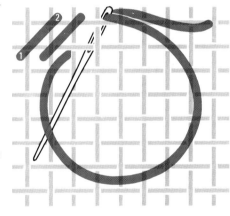

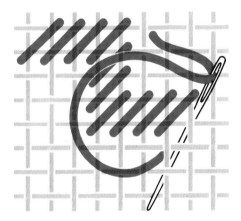

Jacquard stitch. Here, too, canvas is covered with rows of Byzantine stitches, but rows are spaced one mesh apart, leaving stepped rows of blank meshes. On each row of exposed meshes, form tent stitches (p. 15). Work rows from bottom up, turning canvas completely for each new row. On horizontal steps, form stitches in the usual way, bringing needle out at base of stitch (1) and in at top of stitch (2). On vertical steps, reverse the direction of stitch formation, bringing needle out at top of stitch (A) and in at base (B).

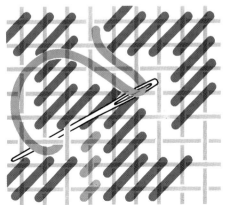

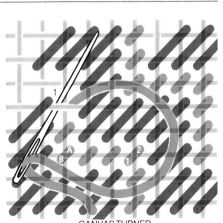

CANVAS TURNED

Canvas work stitches

Diagonal stitches

Mosaic stitch

Condensed mosaic stitch

MOSAIC STITCHES

Mosaic stitch produces a block-like pattern through repetition of the same three stitches. Rows of these stitches can be worked either horizontally or diagonally across the canvas. When only one thread colour is used, both methods result in the same pattern; when two colours are used, because the colours are differently placed with each method, the resulting patterns will differ greatly (p. 54). Condensed mosaic stitch produces an overall texture by repeating the same two stitches. It is always worked diagonally. Use mosaic and condensed mosaic stitches in small or large areas.

Mosaic stitch (done horizontally). Begin at upper right; work rows right to left. Each is a repeated grouping of three stitches worked to form blocks. Form block as follows: work one tent stitch, 1 to 2; next, a longer stitch across two canvas meshes, 3 to 4, then another tent stitch, 5 to 6. Begin next block one canvas hole to the left. At end of each row, leave needle at back of canvas, then turn canvas completely around. Align blocks of new row with blocks of preceding row.

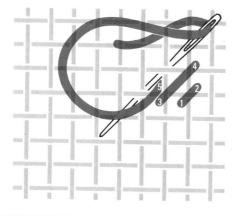

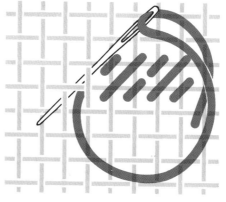

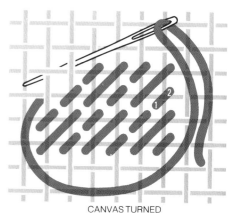

CANVAS TURNED

Mosaic stitch (done diagonally). Start at upper left and work first row diagonally down to lower right. Work successive rows alternately up, then down the canvas, filling in first the upper, then the lower areas. Each row is a repeated formation of mosaic stitch blocks (1 to 6), but blocks are placed diagonally next to each other, missing one canvas hole between. At end of row, reverse working direction and fit new blocks between blocks of preceding row.

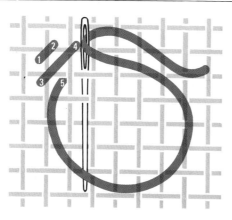

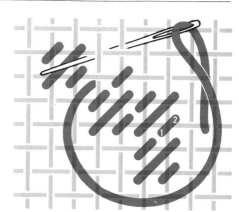

Condensed mosaic stitch.
Start at upper left; work first row diagonally to lower right. Work subsequent rows up, then down canvas; fill in first upper, then lower areas. For each row, alternately form a tent stitch, 1 to 2, then one stitch diagonally across two meshes, 3 to 4. Form the next tent stitch over the mesh opposite the centre of the 3–4 stitch. At end of each row, change working direction; place new stitches so that the tent stitches are next to the long stitches of preceding row.

Scotch stitch

Condensed Scotch stitch

Chequer stitch

SCOTCH STITCHES

Like mosaic stitch, Scotch stitch can be worked horizontally or diagonally across the canvas to produce a block-like pattern. Blocks are formed, however, of five rather than three stitches. Condensed Scotch stitch is always worked diagonally: it repeats a group of four rather than five stitches. There is also a variation of Scotch stitch called chequer stitch. It alternates blocks of Scotch stitches with same-size blocks of tent stitches (diagonal tent stitches here). Scotch stitches, being slightly larger than mosaic stitches, cannot fit into as small a canvas area.

Scotch stitch (done horizontally). Start at upper right; work each row from right to left. Each row is a repeated group of five stitches worked to form blocks. For each block: form a tent stitch, 1 to 2, then a stitch over two meshes, 3 to 4, follow with stitch over three meshes, 5 to 6, another over two, 7 to 8, then a tent stitch, 9 to 10. Place next block to left of this. At each row's end, turn canvas around; place new blocks in line with those of preceding row.

CANVAS TURNED

Canvas work stitches

Diagonal stitches

Scotch stitch (done diagonally). Start at upper left and work first row diagonally to lower right. Work the remaining rows alternately up, then down canvas, first filling in upper right, then lower left. Each row consists of blocks of Scotch stitches (1 to 10). Place blocks diagonally next to each other with one canvas hole missed between blocks. At the end of each row, reverse working direction and fit blocks of new row into indentations in preceding row.

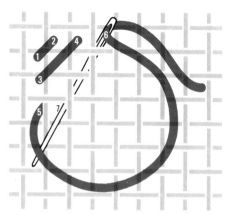  

Condensed Scotch stitch. Start at upper left and work first row diagonally to lower right. Work subsequent rows up, then down the canvas to fill in first the upper, then the lower halves. For each row, repeat the following four stitches: a tent stitch, 1 to 2, a stitch over two meshes, 3 to 4, another over three meshes, 5 to 6, a fourth over two meshes, 7 to 8. Start new repeat over mesh opposite centre of last stitch. At end of each row, change working direction; form new tent stitches next to longest stitches of preceding row.

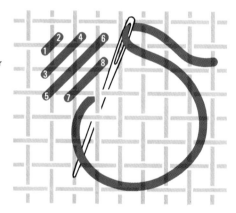 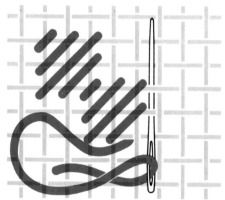 

Chequer stitch. Start at upper right; work each row right to left. Each row alternates a block of Scotch stitches with a block of tent stitches. Start with a block of Scotch stitches; next to it, work a block of tent stitches to cover same area (three by three meshes). Diagonal tent stitches (p. 15) used here are formed in the order indicated by the letters A to I. At the end of each chequer-stitch row, turn the canvas around; align new tent-stitch blocks with the Scotch-stitch blocks of the preceding row.

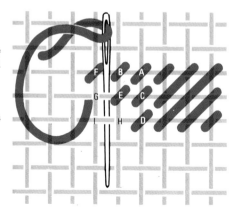 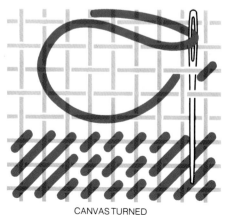 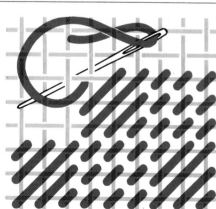

CANVAS TURNED   CANVAS TURNED

20

Cashmere stitch

Condensed cashmere stitch

CASHMERE STITCHES

Cashmere stitches, like mosaic and Scotch stitches, form a block-like pattern on the canvas. The blocks in this case, however, are rectangular, not square like those formed with the other two stitch types. Each block of cashmere stitches consists of four stitches; rows of cashmere stitches can be worked either horizontally or diagonally across the canvas. In the condensed cashmere stitch, each repeat is three stitches; the rows are always worked diagonally. Cashmere stitches can be used in most parts of a canvas work design, but they are especially good for backgrounds.

Cashmere stitch (done horizontally). Start at upper right and work each row from right to left. Each row consists of rectangular blocks that are formed by identical groups of four stitches. Form each group of stitches as follows: work a tent stitch, 1 to 2, two long stitches, each over two meshes, 3 to 4 and 5 to 6, then another tent stitch, 7 to 8. Place the next block to the left of this. At the end of each row, turn canvas around; align new rectangular blocks with those of the row just completed.

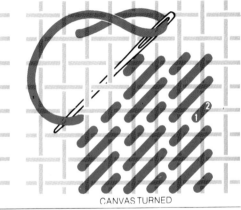

CANVAS TURNED

Cashmere stitch (done diagonally). Work first row of stitches from upper left corner diagonally down to lower right. Work subsequent rows alternately up, then down canvas, filling in first upper right, then lower left areas. Each row is made up of units of cashmere stitches (1 to 8). Each unit is placed diagonally next to the other, with one canvas hole missed in between. At the end of each row, reverse the working direction and fit new units into indentations made by units of the preceding row.

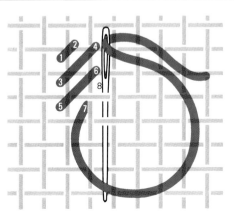

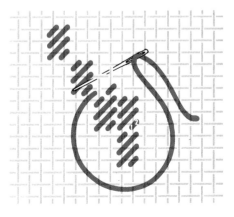

Canvas work stitches

Diagonal stitches

Condensed cashmere stitch.
Start first row at upper left; work to lower right. Successive rows are worked alternately up, then down the canvas first to cover upper right, then lower left areas of canvas. Each row is a repeated series of the same three-stitch unit: one tent stitch, 1 to 2, then two long stitches each over two meshes, 3 to 4 and 5 to 6. Start next unit over mesh that is opposite last stitch. At end of each row, change direction; fit new units into indentations formed by preceding row.

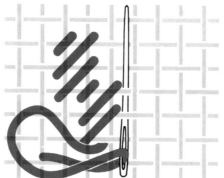

Milanese stitch

Oriental stitch

MILANESE STITCHES
Both Milanese stitch and its variation, Oriental stitch, form large and very dramatic patterns on canvas. Neither stitch should be used for a small area. Milanese stitch is composed of rows of triangular units of stitches. Oriental stitch starts with rows of Milanese stitches, but these rows are spaced to allow for the addition of groups of long diagonal stitches. When all rows of the Oriental stitch are done in one colour, a large, stepped pattern develops. But when the rows are done in alternating colours, the two different patterns frame one another (see left).

Milanese stitch.
Work first row diagonally, upper left to lower right. Do subsequent rows up, then down canvas; fill in upper, then lower areas. Each row is a repetition of a group of four stitches worked to form triangular units. For each unit, form one tent stitch, 1 to 2, then a stitch over two meshes, 3 to 4, another over three meshes, 5 to 6, the last over four meshes, 7 to 8. Start next unit over mesh opposite centre of last stitch. At each row's end, change direction. Form new tent stitches diagonally next to longest stitches of previous row; reverse direction of triangular units.

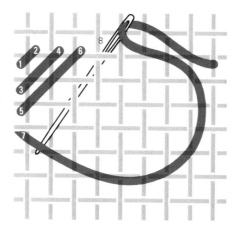
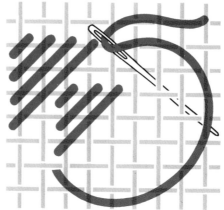
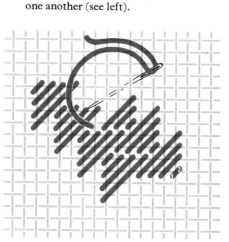

Oriental stitch. Begin by laying down rows of Milanese stitches in the following manner. Starting at upper left, work rows down, then up the canvas, filling in first upper, then lower halves. Reverse direction of the triangular units with each row. Space these rows so that the longest stitches of all units lie next to each other diagonally. This particular row-to-row arrangement of the units leaves open rectangular areas of canvas between the rows; direction of the open areas alternates from vertical in one row to horizontal in the next.

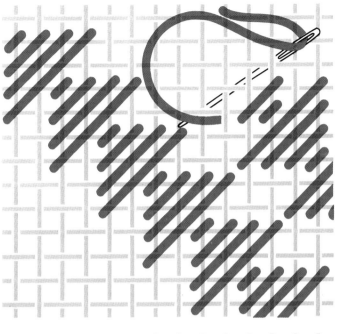

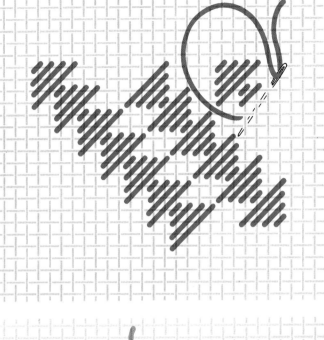

Fill in the open areas as follows: starting with the first open space in the upper left corner, work the rows diagonally down, then up the canvas. Work the vertically shaped rows down the canvas; those that are horizontal, up the canvas. In every area, form three diagonal stitches, each over two meshes, 1 to 2. Form stitches in the vertical areas below one another; place the stitches in horizontal areas next to each other. All of the stitches should slant in the same direction, from lower left to upper right. All groups of stitches hug the edges of Milanese stitches. When using filling-in stitches (p. 55) to complete the outer edges of the stitched area, maintain the pattern of separate rows of stitches.

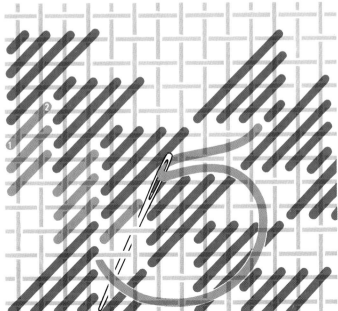

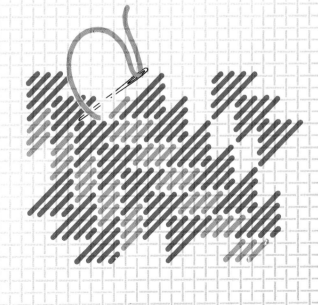

Canvas work stitches

Diagonal stitches

Kelim stitch

Stem stitch

KELIM STITCHES

Kelim stitch and its variation, stem stitch, form plait-like patterns on the canvas. The pattern that emerges from Kelim stitch, as shown here, travels across the canvas; stem stitch pattern goes up and down. Both patterns are composed of rows of diagonal stitches, with the stitches in each successive row slanted the opposite way from the stitches in the preceding row. Stem stitch also involves backstitches between paired rows of diagonal stitches. Both Kelim and stem stitches can be used for small or large design areas; Kelim stitch is suitable for use in rugs.

Kelim stitch. Begin at upper right and work rows alternately from right to left, then left to right. Each stitch is taken over one horizontal by two vertical canvas threads. When working rows from right to left, bring needle out at base of stitch, 1, and in at top of stitch, 2. When working rows from left to right, reverse the slant of the stitches by bringing the needle out at top of stitch, 3, and in at base of stitch, 4. Rows of stitches are formed directly below one another.

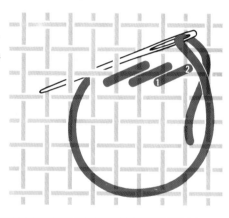
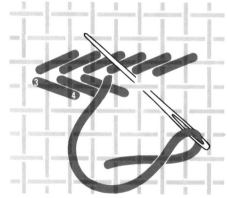
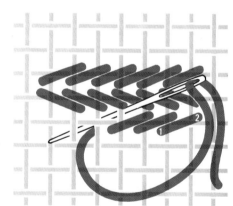

Stem stitch. Start at upper left and work in groups of three rows. One row of diagonal stitches is worked down the canvas, a second up; a third row, of backstitches (see p. 32), is worked down the canvas, between the first two rows. Form each diagonal stitch over two meshes. When working stitches down the canvas, slant them up to the left, 1 to 2; when going up the canvas, slant them up to the right, 3 to 4. Work a backstitch, A to B, over every horizontal thread between bases of diagonal stitches. Form next repeat to right.

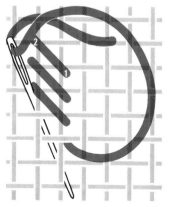

Straight stitches

The stitches in this group are called straight stitches because all of them, except for the backstitch done diagonally, are formed to lie parallel to the threads of the canvas. In most instances, the stitches are parallel to the vertical canvas threads. Two exceptions are darning stitch and backstitch done hori zontally; these lie parallel to the horizontal threads. The straight-stitch group also includes Florentine stitch and its variations. These produce the familiar zigzag stitch patterns that are associated with Florentine work. The techniques for this are explained in more detail starting on p. 67.

STRAIGHT GOBELIN STITCHES

Straight Gobelin and encroaching straight Gobelin stitches are comparable in their formation, but not in the patterns they produce. The visual difference is caused by the way the rows of stitches are placed. Straight Gobelin stitches result in a definite row-by-row pattern because each row of stitches is separate from the other. Encroaching straight Gobelin stitches form a uniform texture because the rows overlap. Both stitches can be varied in length (see below) to suit canvas areas of any size.

Straight Gobelin stitch

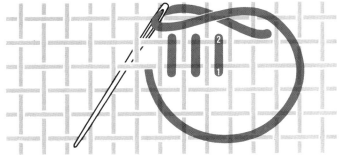 

Encroaching straight Gobelin stitch

Straight Gobelin stitch. Start at upper right; work rows alternately right to left, then left to right. For each stitch, bring needle out at 1, pass it up over the canvas, down into 2. Space between 1 and 2 can be from two to five horizontal threads. Spacing here is two horizontal threads. At the end of each row, reverse working direction; place new stitches so their bases (1) are one stitch length below bases of stitches in preceding row.

Encroaching straight Gobelin stitch. Start at upper right and work rows alternately right to left, then left to right. For each stitch, bring needle out at 1, pass it up over the canvas, down into 2. Space between 1 and 2 can vary as for straight Gobelin stitches. Space shown here is three horizontal canvas threads. At each row's end, reverse working direction. Position tops (2) of new stitches one horizontal thread above, but consistently to the left or right of the bases of the stitches in preceding row (tops here are to the left).

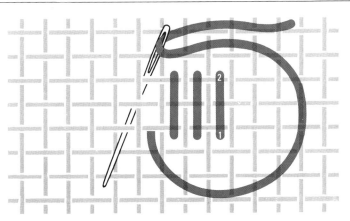 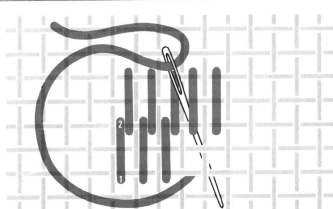

Canvas work stitches

Straight stitches

Brick stitch

Gobelin filling stitch

BRICK STITCHES

Brick stitch and Gobelin filling stitch are alike in that each produces a very similar pattern. Each individual brick stitch, however, is only two canvas threads long, whereas each Gobelin filling stitch is six threads long. Another similarity between the two is that the methods of ·row formation (shown below for both of the stitches) are interchangeable. The row method illustrated for the brick stitch produces single rows of stitches, each of which forms a zigzag pattern across the canvas. With the row method that is shown for Gobelin filling stitch, this same zigzag effect is produced after two rows.

Brick stitch. Starting at upper right, work rows alternately right to left, then left to right. Each row makes use of three horizontal canvas threads, but each stitch spans only two of these threads. Position of stitches alternates in each row, first being over the top two threads, then over the lower two. For each stitch, bring needle out at 1, insert at 2. At each row's end, reverse working direction. Position bases (1) of new stitches one stitch length below bases of stitches in preceding row.

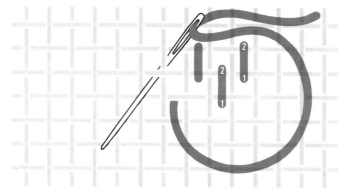

Gobelin filling stitch. Start at upper right and work rows alternately from right to left, then left to right. For each stitch, bring needle out at 1, up over six horizontal canvas threads, then down into 2. Position bases (1) of stitches one canvas hole apart. At the end of each row, reverse working direction. Position new stitches so that their top halves are between the stitches of the preceding row.

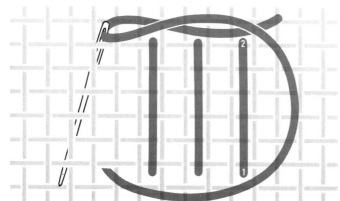

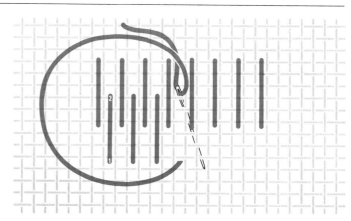

Florentine stitch

Two variations of Florentine stitch

FLORENTINE STITCHES

Florentine stitch and its variations form the zigzag patterns used so often in the type of canvas work known as Florentine embroidery. The high points of the zigzag are referred to as peaks, the low points as valleys. Each row consists of straight stitches placed next to each other in a diagonal arrangement up and down the canvas. The diagonal effect results from the 'step' between stitches. **Step** is the term for the number of horizontal canvas threads between the bases of neighbouring stitches. A kind of shorthand is used to specify stitch length and step. Given as two numbers separated by a full stop, for example, 3.1, the first number means stitch length, the second number stands for the step between the stitches. The amount of step is always less than the length of the stitch. The pattern of a Florentine stitch is arrived at by manipulating the number, length and steps of the stitches. In its basic form, Florentine stitch has an even peak-and-valley pattern. Two variations are shown here. For more on Florentine stitches, see p. 67.

Florentine stitch. Work first row in two movements across horizontal centre of canvas, from vertical centre to left, then from centre to right. Work subsequent rows in one movement, from right edge to left, or left to right. Place rows above or below first row, fitting stitches of each new row into jagged edge of preceding row. Overall pattern is usually a repeat of several rows; three-row repeat is shown here with second two above the first. In each row, there can be from three to eight stitches between valley and peaks (four shown). Stitches can be two to eight horizontal canvas threads long; step must be at least one less than the stitch-length number. Stitches in all of these rows are four threads long with step of two between stitches (4.2).

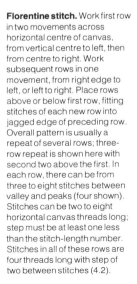

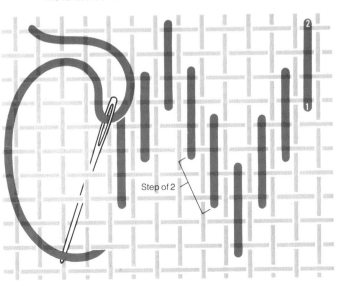

Step of 2

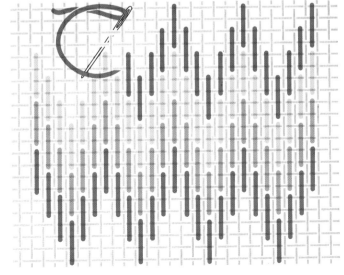

Canvas work stitches

Straight stitches

One way to vary Florentine stitch is to work rows that form peaks and valleys of varying sizes. This general pattern of uneven points is called flame stitch. There is no set pattern; you can design your own. In general, the more stitches used between peak and valley, the longer those stitches, and the greater the step between stitches, the higher the point will be. Usually, the stitches of any one row are the same length; the step between them can vary to give an even more undulating look to the row. The stitch length used for each subsequent row can be different from the first, but the step plan established by the first row should be maintained. On the immediate right the first row is being done; in the compressed drawing, far right, the first row is the centre row. Notice how the step change is maintained even though a different stitch length is used for each row.

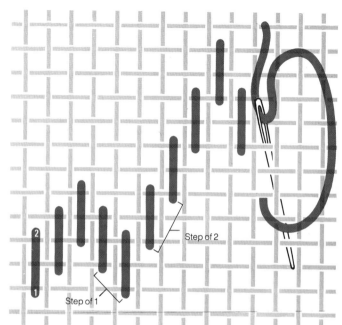

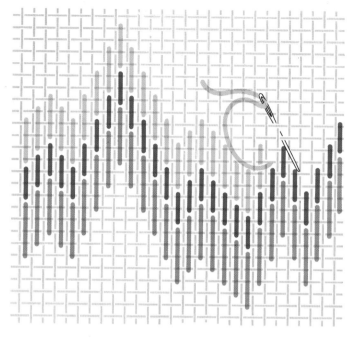

Another way to vary Florentine stitches is to round off the peaks (and valleys, not shown). This is achieved through the use of blocks of stitches. There can be two or more (usually up to six) in each block. The number of blocks used to round off the point can vary. In general, the more blocks used, and the more stitches in each block, the rounder the point will be. The stitches in each block are the same length; the step between blocks can vary with the length of stitch used. The row pattern can include pointed and rounded peaks and valleys. The block and step plan established by the first row (top row in compressed drawing) is maintained by the other two. It is not necessary, however, for the stitch length to be the same in each row.

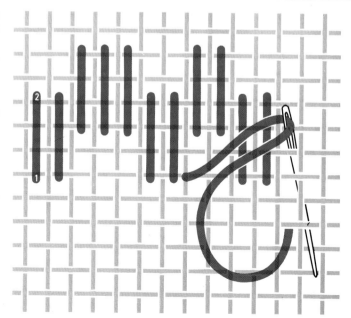

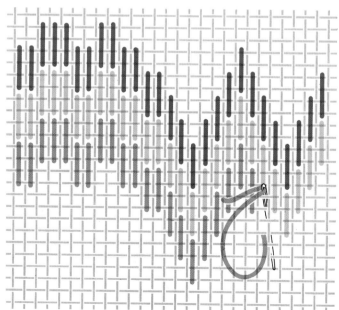

Hungarian stitch

Hungarian diamond stitch

Hungarian grounding

HUNGARIAN STITCHES

Both Hungarian stitch and Hungarian diamond stitch produce patterns of diamond-shaped units across the canvas. Each of the diamond-shaped units of Hungarian stitch is small and consists of three stitches. The diamonds of Hungarian diamond stitch are larger because each unit consists of five stitches. The pattern of Hungarian grounding is achieved by alternating rows of Hungarian stitches with rows of Florentine stitches. Any of these stitches is excellent for filling in large or background areas of a canvas work design.

Hungarian stitch. Start at upper right; work rows alternately right to left, left to right. Each row is a repeated grouping of three stitches to form diamond-shaped units. For each unit, work one stitch over two horizontal canvas threads, 1 to 2, next a stitch over four threads, 3 to 4, then another over two threads, 5 to 6. Miss one canvas hole to start next unit. At each row's end, reverse direction; work new units so tops of long stitches are between units of preceding row.

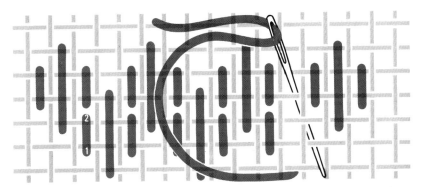

Hungarian diamond stitch. Begin at upper right and work rows alternately right to left, then left to right. Each row is a repeated grouping of five stitches to form large diamond-shaped units. Form each unit as follows: work one straight stitch over two horizontal canvas threads, 1 to 2, a longer stitch over four threads, 3 to 4, another over six threads, 5 to 6, followed by a stitch over four threads, 7 to 8, then another over two threads, 9 to 10. Miss one canvas hole to start next unit. At end of each row, reverse working direction. Position new diamond units so that the tops of the longest stitches fall between the diamonds of the preceding row.

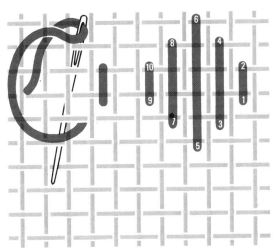
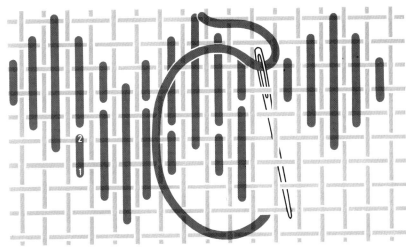

Canvas work stitches

Straight stitches

Hungarian grounding. Start by working a row of Florentine stitches across centre of canvas (p. 27). Form its even peaks and valleys three stitches deep, using stitches four threads long with a step of one between them. Then work a row of Hungarian stitches, placing longest stitches of each unit below the peaks of the Florentine. Below this, work a row of Florentine, placing its valleys below longest stitches of the Hungarian-stitch units. Continue alternating stitch rows; turn canvas to stitch open area of canvas in the same way.

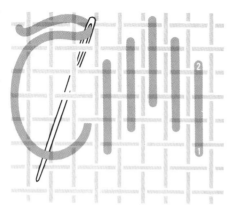
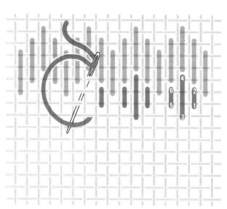
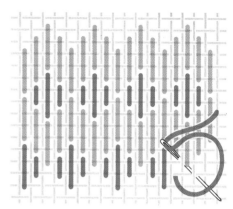

Parisian stitch

Old Florentine stitch

PARISIAN STITCHES

Parisian stitch forms an irregular texture across the canvas; old Florentine stitch produces a very large pattern resembling the surface of a woven basket. The size difference between these two patterns is caused by the size of the individual stitches, Parisian stitches being shorter than old Florentine. The row structure for both Parisian and old Florentine stitches is very similar (see below and facing page). Stitches in each row of Parisian alternate from one short to one long stitch; stitches in each row of old Florentine alternate two short stitches with two that are very long.

Parisian stitch. Start at upper right and work rows alternately right to left, then left to right. For each row, alternately form a short stitch over two horizontal canvas threads, 1 to 2, then a long stitch over four threads, 3 to 4. At end of each row, reverse working direction. Position new stitches so that the tops (2) of the short stitches are in the same canvas hole as the bases of the long stitches in the preceding row.

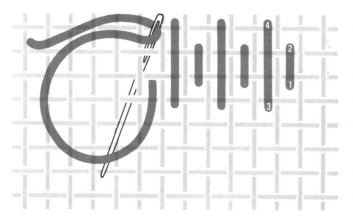
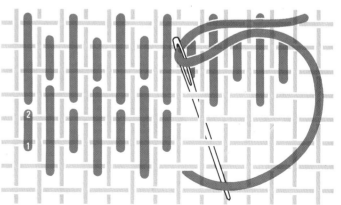

Old Florentine stitch. Start at upper right; work rows alternately from right to left, then left to right. For each row, alternately form two short, then two long stitches. Work each short stitch over three horizontal canvas threads, 1 to 2 and 3 to 4; form each long stitch over nine threads, 5 to 6 and 7 to 8. At end of each row, reverse working direction. Position new stitches so that the tops of the short stitches (2 and 4) are in the same canvas holes as the bases of the long stitches of the preceding row.

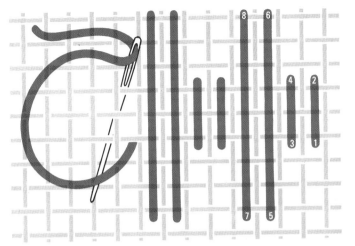 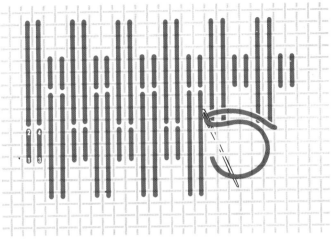

Darning stitch

Enlargement of darning stitch

DARNING STITCH

Darning stitch produces a very tightly stitched surface on the canvas. For each row of darning stitches, the thread is woven across the canvas in four journeys (complete spans) to form interlocking long and short stitches within the space of two horizontal canvas threads. The sample has been enlarged to make the stitches easier to see.

Darning stitch. Work each row in four journeys (full spans) across the canvas, within the space of two horizontal canvas threads. Starting at upper left, work first journey to the right, forming long stitches as follows: bring needle out at 1, over four vertical threads (1 to 2) then under two (2 to 1). At end of journey, reverse direction. Work second journey to the left, forming short stitches as follows: with needle out at 1, pass over two vertical threads (1 to 2) then under four (2 to 1). Work third journey like the first; work the fourth like the second. Form the next set of journeys between the next two horizontal canvas threads (1).

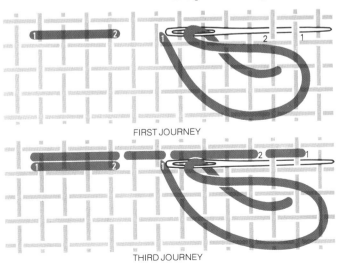 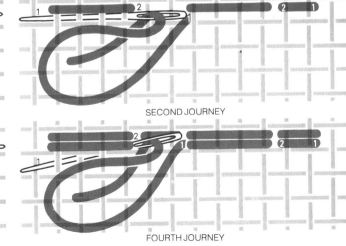

FIRST JOURNEY

SECOND JOURNEY

THIRD JOURNEY

FOURTH JOURNEY

Canvas work stitches

Straight stitches

Backstitch (done horizontally)

Backstitch (done vertically)

Backstitch (done diagonally)

BACKSTITCHES

In canvas work, backstitches are never used to cover an entire area of blank canvas. Rather, they are used as single rows of stitches to outline a stitched area of a canvas work design, or to cover the canvas threads left exposed by another canvas work stitch (see diamond eyelet, p. 47). They can be worked in all directions on the canvas.

Backstitch (done horizontally). Work rows either right to left or left to right. When working right to left, point needle to left; when working left to right, point needle to right. For each stitch, bring needle out at 1, pass it back over one vertical thread, into 2. To start next stitch, pass needle under two vertical threads.

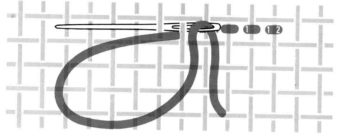

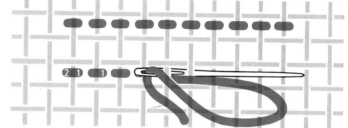

Backstitch (done vertically). Rows can be worked down or up the canvas. When working down, have needle pointing down; when working up, have needle pointing up. Form each stitch as follows: bring needle out at 1, pass it back over one horizontal canvas thread, then into 2. Pass needle under two horizontal threads to start the next stitch.

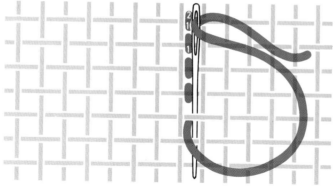

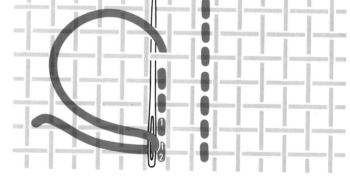

Backstitch (done diagonally). Rows can be worked diagonally up or down the canvas, to span canvas right to left, as shown, or left to right. When working down, have needle pointing down; when working up, have needle pointing up. For each stitch, bring needle out at 1, pass it back over one mesh, into 2. Pass needle under two meshes to start next stitch.

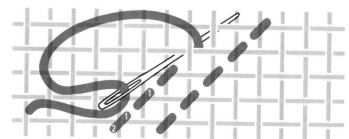

Crossing stitches

The stitches in this group are classified as crossing stitches because each of their patterns is achieved through the use of stitches that cross over each other. Some stitches are diagonal, some straight. Some of the stitches involve only two stitches for each unit; cross stitch is an example. In others, there are more than two, eight in double leviathan stitch, for instance. The crossing of the stitches occurs, for the most part, within each individual unit or within a row of units.

Exceptions are the plaited and perspective stitches; in these two cases, the crossing takes place between two rows of diagonal stitches.

CROSS STITCHES

A cross stitch consists of two diagonal stitches crossing at the centre. Generally a cross stitch spans only one canvas mesh, and its upper stitch slants the same as a tent stitch. Cross stitches can be formed in two ways. Use either method to form any size cross stitch on interlock or double canvas; to form one-mesh cross stitches on single canvas, use Method 1 below. To alter the slant of the upper stitch of any cross stitch, see bottom of next page.

Cross stitch with upper stitch slanting same as tent stitch

Cross stitch variation (upper stitch slanting opposite to tent stitch)

Cross stitch (Method 1, done horizontally). Start at upper left; work rows alternately from left to right, then right to left. For each cross stitch, form the lower stitch first, coming out at 1 and going in at 2. Then form the upper stitch, bringing the needle out at 3, up over the 1–2 stitch, then inserting it at 4. At end of each row, reverse working direction and form the new stitch row directly below the stitches just completed.

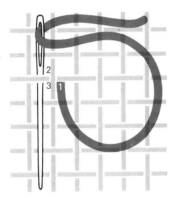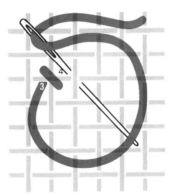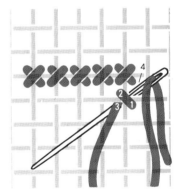

Cross stitch (Method 1, done vertically). Start at upper left; work each row down the canvas. For each cross stitch, form the lower stitch first, coming out at 1, going in at 2. Then form the upper stitch over the lower, coming out at 3 and going in at 4. At end of each row, finish last stitch, but leave needle at back of canvas. Then turn the canvas completely around and form the new row of stitches next to those just completed.

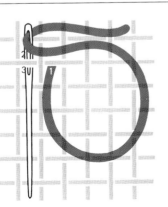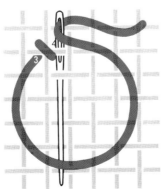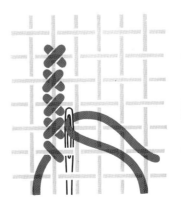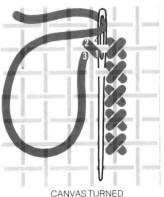

CANVAS TURNED

33

Canvas work stitches

Crossing stitches

Cross stitch (Method 2, done horizontally). Start at upper right; work each row of cross stitches in two spans – first from right to left, then left to right. When working from right to left, form lower stitches of the cross stitches by bringing needle out at 1, inserting at 2. At end of span, reverse work direction. Working from left to right, form the upper stitches of the cross stitches by bringing needle out at 3, over the 1–2 stitch, then in at 4. Work next row of cross stitches below those just completed.

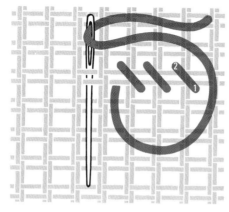 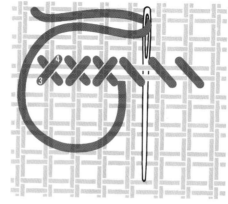 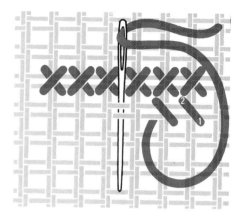

Cross stitch (Method 2, done vertically). Start at upper right; work each row of cross stitches in two spans – first down, then up the canvas. When working down, form the lower stitches of the cross stitches by bringing needle out at 1 and inserting it at 2. At end of span, reverse working direction. Working upwards, form the upper stitches of the cross stitches, bringing needle out at 3 and over 1–2 stitch, then inserting it at 4. Work next row of cross stitches to left of those just completed.

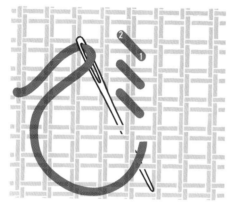  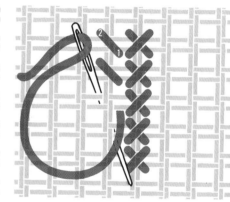

To reverse slant of upper stitch, change way of forming the upper and lower stitches of the cross. The easiest way to understand this is by comparing steps 1 to 2 (the lower stitch) and steps 3 to 4 (the upper stitch) on the right with the 1–2 and 3–4 steps shown above (Method 2) and on preceding page (Method 1). If you use Method 1, the working direction of rows, whether horizontal or vertical, stays the same. With Method 2, reverse directions, starting at upper left to work rows horizontally; at lower left to work rows vertically.

 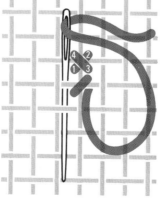 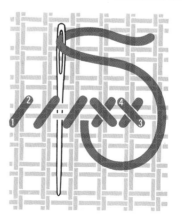 

Oblong cross stitch

Oblong cross stitch with backstitch

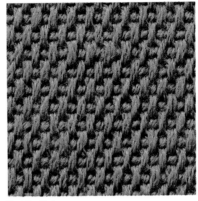

Double stitch

OBLONG CROSS STITCHES

Oblong cross stitch is an elongated cross stitch consisting of two diagonal stitches that cross each other to span a rectangular area of the canvas. All three of the stitch samples shown here use oblong cross stitches either by themselves or in combination with other stitches. First sample is of plain oblong cross stitches. The middle sample is of oblong cross stitches each of which has a backstitch across its centre. The last sample is of double stitch, in which oblong cross stitches alternate with one-mesh cross stitches. For a two-colour version of double stitch, see p. 54.

Oblong cross stitch. Starting at upper right, work each row in two spans across the canvas. First work from right to left, forming lower stitches of each oblong cross stitch, 1 to 2. Space between 1 and 2 is two horizontal by one vertical canvas thread. Then, at end of span, work row back to right, forming upper stitches of each oblong cross stitch, 3 to 4. Space between 3 and 4 is same as between 1 and 2. With each new row, position bases of new stitches (1 and 3) one stitch length below the stitches of the preceding row.

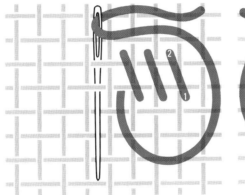 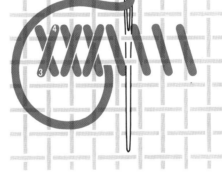 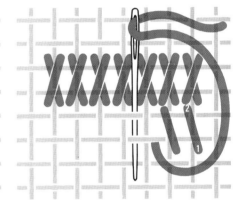

Oblong cross stitch with backstitch. Start at upper right; work rows alternately from right to left, then left to right. For each stitch, form an oblong cross stitch, 1 to 2 and 3 to 4, then work a backstitch over the centre of the cross stitch, 5 to 6. Size of oblong cross stitch is same as above; 5-6 stitch is over one vertical canvas thread. At each row's end, change work direction. Place bases of new stitches (1 and 3) one stitch length below stitches just done; reverse direction of 5 to 6 so a backstitch is formed.

 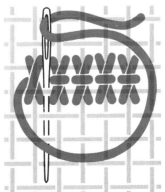 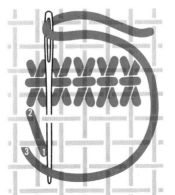 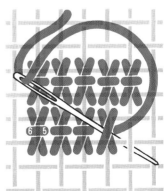

Canvas work stitches

Crossing stitches

Double stitch. Start at upper left and work rows alternately left to right, then right to left. For each row, alternately form oblong and normal cross stitches. Work each oblong cross stitch over three horizontal by one vertical canvas thread, 1 to 2, 3 to 4; work each normal cross stitch over one mesh, 5 to 6, 7 to 8. At end of each row, reverse working direction. Place new stitches so that tops of oblong cross stitches (2 and 4) are in same canvas holes as bases of the normal cross stitches of the preceding row.

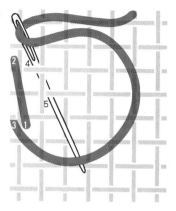   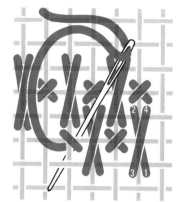

Upright cross stitch

Double cross stitch

UPRIGHT CROSS STITCHES

Each upright cross stitch is composed of two straight stitches that cross at their centres. The lower stitch lies parallel to the vertical threads of the canvas; the upper stitch is parallel to the horizontal canvas threads. By themselves, upright cross stitches produce a pebbly texture on the canvas. Used in combination with large normal cross stitches, they become the double cross stitch pattern. Double cross stitch creates a lovely latticework pattern, which can be made even more interesting by working it in two colours. For two-colour working techniques, see p. 54.

Upright cross stitch. Start at upper left and work rows alternately from left to right, then right to left. For each upright cross stitch, bring needle out at 1, in at 2, then out at 3 and in at 4. Each upright cross stitch can span two or four vertical by horizontal canvas threads (span of two is shown). At each row's end, reverse working direction. Place new stitches so their tops (2) share a canvas hole with neighbouring horizontal stitches in the preceding row.

 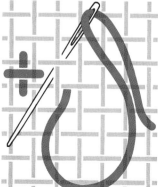  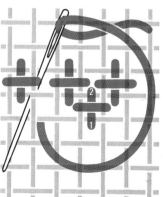

Double cross stitch. Start at upper left; work rows left to right, then right to left. For each row, alternately form a large cross stitch to span four by four canvas threads, 1 to 2 and 3 to 4; then form an upright cross stitch over two by two threads, 5 to 6 and 7 to 8. At each row's end, change work direction. Place tops of new large cross stitches (2 and 4) in canvas holes of bases of large cross stitches in preceding row. Cover canvas with double cross stitch; form upright cross stitches between rows (A to B and C to·D).

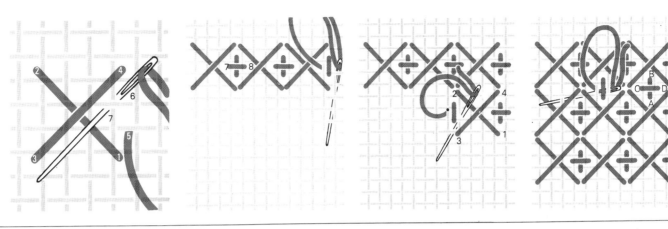

Double straight cross stitch

Leviathan stitch

Double leviathan stitch

DOUBLE STRAIGHT CROSS STITCH/ LEVIATHAN STITCHES

All three of the patterns in this group form large, raised stitch units, each consisting of multiple layers of crossing stitches and spanning four horizontal by four vertical canvas threads. The resulting units, however, are different in shape. Units of the double straight cross stitch are diamond-shaped; those of both the leviathan and double leviathan stitches are square. These are very precise stitches, and to achieve their neat layering and distinctive look, you must follow the sequence of steps with great care.

Double straight cross stitch.
Start at upper left and work rows left to right, then right to left. Form each stitch as follows: first, a large upright cross stitch that spans four by four canvas threads, 1 to 2 and 3 to 4; then, a large cross stitch, over centre of upright cross stitch, spanning two by two threads, 5 to 6 and 7 to 8. Miss three canvas holes between bases (1) of stitches. At each row's end, change work direction. Place new stitches so that tops (2) share canvas hole with neighbouring horizontal stitches in row above.

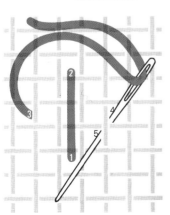

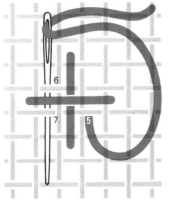

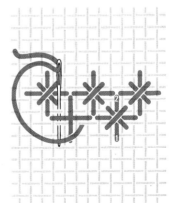

Canvas work stitches

Crossing stitches

Leviathan stitch (also known as double cross stitch and Smyrna stitch). Start at upper left and work rows from left to right, then right to left. Form each stitch as follows: first, a large cross stitch that spans four by four canvas threads, 1 to 2 and 3 to 4; then, a large upright cross stitch, over centre of large cross stitch, that spans four by four threads, 5 to 6 and 7 to 8. At end of each row, reverse work direction. Place new stitches so tops (2, 6 and 4) share canvas holes with bases of stitches in row above.

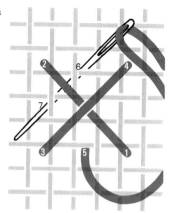
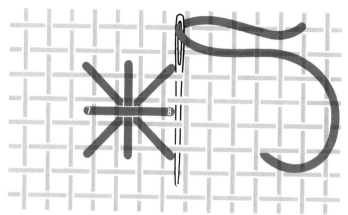
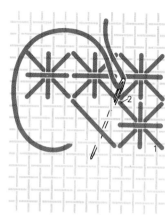

Double leviathan stitch. Start at upper left; work rows alternately left to right, then right to left. For each stitch, first form a large cross stitch over four by four canvas threads, 1 to 2 and 3 to 4. Then bring needle out at 5, up over the cross stitch and in at 6, out at 7. Pass needle down over cross stitch, in at 8, out at 9. Bring needle up over cross stitch, in at 10, out at 11. Pass needle down over cross stitch, in at 12, out at 13.

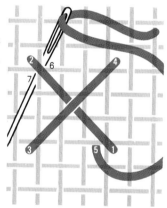
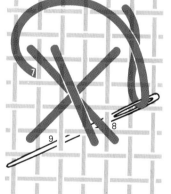
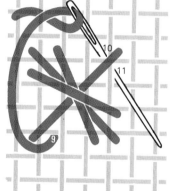
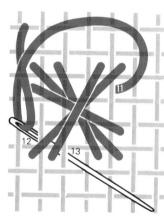

To complete the stitch, form a large upright cross stitch as follows: bring needle from 13 up over the stitch and in at 14; then, out at 15, across the stitch, and in at 16. At the end of each row, reverse the working direction. Position stitches of new row so their tops (2, 6, 14, 10 and 4) share canvas holes with the bases of the stitches in the row just completed.

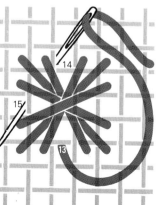
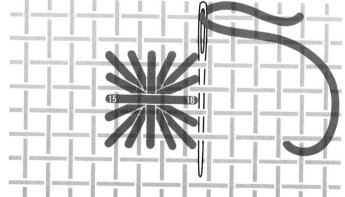

Knotted stitch

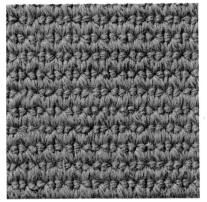
French stitch

Rococo stitch

KNOTTED STITCHES

These three patterns – knotted stitch, French stitch and rococo stitch – all involve long stitches that are held down to the canvas by short crossing stitches. In knotted stitch, both the long and the short stitches cross diagonally over each other and over the canvas. In the French and rococo stitch patterns, long straight stitches are crossed by short straight stitches, but the long straight stitches become bowed in shape when the short crossing stitches have anchored them to the canvas. Of the three knotted types, the rococo stitch pattern is the largest and most dramatic.

Knotted stitch. Start at upper right; work rows alternately right to left, left to right. For each stitch, bring needle out at 1, over three horizontal and one vertical canvas thread, in at 2. Bring needle out at 3, over the 1–2 stitch, and in at 4. When working rows from right to left, work 3–4 stitch down over 1–2 stitch; working left to right, work 3–4 stitch up over 1–2 stitch. At each row's end, change working direction. Place tops of new stitches (2) one canvas hole above and to the right of bases of stitches just done.

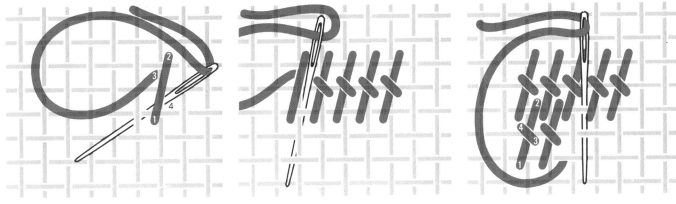

French stitch. Begin at upper right; work rows from right to left, then left to right. For each French stitch, form two tied-down straight stitches, both within the space of two vertical canvas threads. Work first stitch, 1 to 2 and 3 to 4; then second, 5 to 6 and 7 to 8. Start next stitch in second canvas hole from base of stitch just done. At each row's end, reverse working direction for rows and for horizontal stitches. Place new stitches between those of row above, so that their tops share canvas hole of neighbouring horizontal stitches.

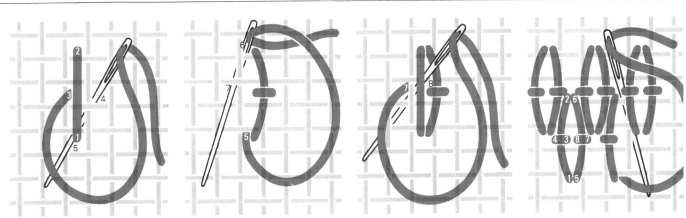

Canvas work stitches

Crossing stitches

Rococo stitch. Begin upper right; work rows from right to left, then left to right. For each rococo stitch, form four tied-down straight stitches, all within the space of two vertical canvas threads, but fanned to span four threads. Work as shown, starting with the first stitch, 1 to 2 and 3 to 4, then the second, 5 to 6, 7 to 8, the third, 9 to 10, 11 to 12, then the fourth, 13 to 14, 15 to 16. Start next stitch in fourth canvas hole from base of stitch just done. Work new rows as shown (explained in French stitch, p. 39).

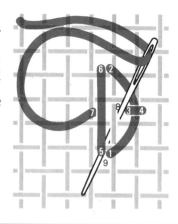
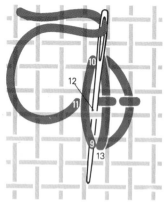
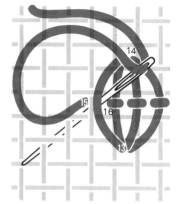
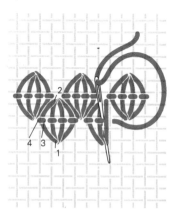

Rice stitch

Enlargement of rice stitch

RICE STITCH

Rice stitch produces a very tightly stitched, well-covered canvas area. Each stitch unit consists of one large ordinary cross stitch and four additional small stitches, each of which crosses a corner of the larger base cross stitch. The sample on the far left shows rice stitches actual size; in the sample on the immediate left, an area of those stitches has been enlarged to show the pattern more clearly. If you wish, rice stitch can be worked in two colours, the large cross stitches first in one colour, then the smaller crossing stitches in the other (see p. 54 for two-colour techniques).

Rice stitch. Start at upper right; work rows alternately right to left, then left to right. For each rice stitch, first work a large cross stitch over two horizontal by two vertical canvas threads, 1 to 2 and 3 to 4. Form four small crossing stitches, each over a corner of the large cross stitch, 5 to 6, 7 to 8, 9 to 10 and 11 to 12. At end of each row, reverse working direction. Place new stitch units directly below those just completed.

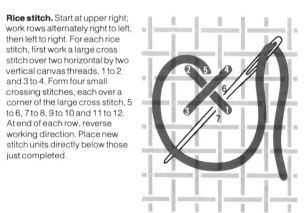

Fishbone stitch

Fern stitch

FISHBONE STITCH/FERN STITCH

Though these stitch patterns are different in result – the fishbone stitch produces a wavy pattern across the canvas, the fern stitch up-and-down stripes – they are quite similar in technique. Both are worked in vertical rows; stitches in each row are crossed, this time off centre. The rows of fishbone stitching are worked alternately down and then up the canvas; all fern stitch rows are worked down. Each fishbone stitch consists of a long diagonal stitch crossed at one end by a short crossing stitch. Fern stitch is made up of two stitches that cross one another at their lower ends.

Fishbone stitch. Start at upper left and work rows down, then up the canvas. Each fishbone stitch consists of a long diagonal stitch that is crossed at one end by a short diagonal stitch. Each long stitch is over three horizontal and two vertical canvas threads; each short stitch is over one mesh. When working row down, work long stitch up, 1 to 2, and cross its top, 3 to 4. When working up a row, work long stitch down, 5 to 6, and cross its bottom, 7 to 8. Rows of stitches are formed next to each other.

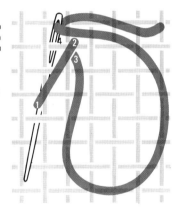
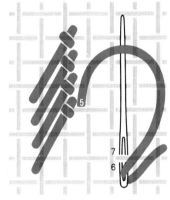

Fern stitch. Start at upper left; work all rows down the canvas. For each stitch, bring needle out at 1, down over two canvas meshes and in at 2; pass under one vertical thread, out at 3, up over two meshes and in at 4. Begin next stitch in canvas hole below the start of the stitch above (1). Form next row of stitches to the right of those just done.

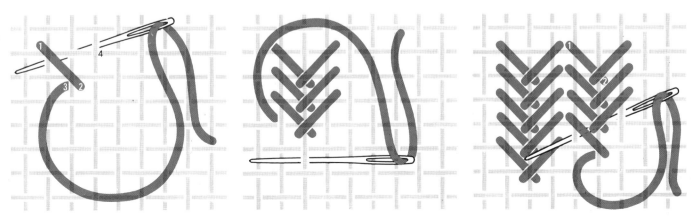

Canvas work stitches

Crossing stitches

Herringbone stitch

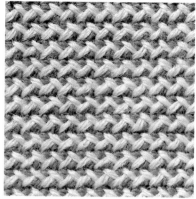
Double herringbone stitch

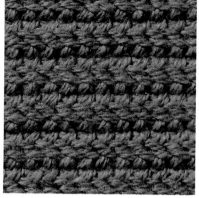
Greek stitch

HERRINGBONE STITCHES/ GREEK STITCH

Both herringbone stitch and its variation, double herringbone stitch, form a tightly woven texture on the canvas. Greek stitch produces a plait-like pattern. All three of these stitch patterns are worked in rows across the canvas; all rows consist of stitches that cross off centre. Both of the herringbone stitches are strong enough to be suitable choices for rugmaking. Greek stitch, however, is not as durable. Double herringbone stitch is usually worked in two contrasting colours as shown on the left and explained below.

Herringbone stitch. Start at upper left; work all rows left to right. Consistently form stitches as follows: bring needle out at 1, down over two canvas meshes and in at 2; then under one vertical thread, out at 3, up over two meshes and in at 4. Pass needle back under one vertical thread to start next stitch. Begin each new row of stitches in the canvas hole below the start of the stitches in the row above.

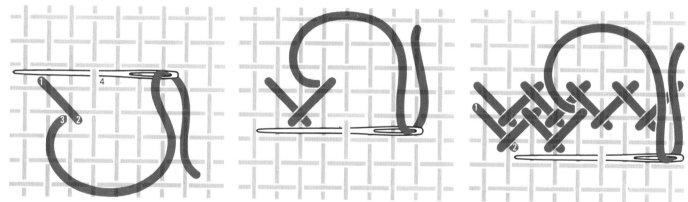

Double herringbone stitch. Begin at upper left; work all rows left to right. Cover the entire canvas area with rows of herringbone stitches (above) but space them by beginning each new row in second canvas hole below the start of the row above. Then go back and cover each of these rows with rows of 'upside-down' herringbone stitches. Bring needle out at A, up over two canvas meshes, in at B; then back under one vertical thread, out at C, down over two meshes, in at D. Pass needle under a vertical thread to start next stitch.

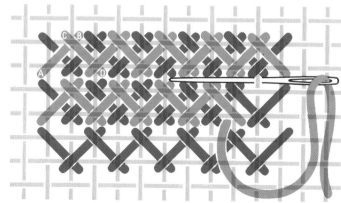

Greek stitch. Begin at upper left; work all rows from left to right. Form each stitch as follows: bring needle out at 1, up over two canvas meshes and in at 2; then under two vertical threads, out at 3, and down into 4, the fourth canvas hole from start of stitch. Pass needle under two vertical threads to begin next stitch. End each row with a 1–2 stitch, then turn canvas completely around to work the next row of stitches. Start each row with a 1–2 stitch.

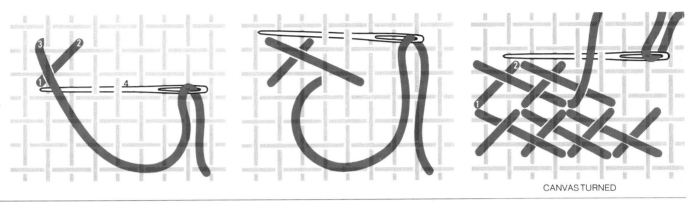

CANVAS TURNED

Plaited stitch

Perspective stitch

PLAITED STITCH/PERSPECTIVE STITCH

Plaited and perspective stitches are unique in the way that their individual stitches cross each other. With these two stitch patterns, the crossing of the stitches does not occur within single rows of stitches. Instead, the stitches of one row become crossed by the formation of the stitches in the next row. Plaited stitch produces the texture of a thick, woven fabric; perspective stitch results in a pattern of three-dimensional boxes. The three-dimensional effect is strongest when done in varying tones of a single colour.

Plaited stitch. Start at upper right and work rows right to left, then left to right. For each stitch, bring needle out at 1, up over four horizontal and two vertical canvas threads, then in at 2. Start next stitch in second canvas hole from base (1) of stitch just done. When working rows right to left, slant stitches back towards the right; when working left to right, slant stitches to the left. At each row's end, change working direction. Position new stitches so their tops (2) are in second canvas hole above bases of stitches just done.

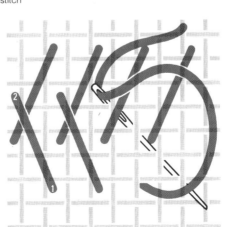
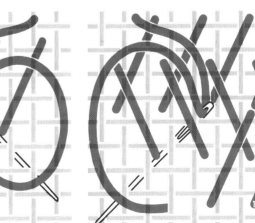

Canvas work stitches

Crossing stitches

Perspective stitch. Worked in series of four rows, each consisting of vertical groups of three diagonal stitches. Each stitch is over two canvas meshes; the working direction, and the slant of the stitches, alternate from group to group. Usually worked in contrasting colours as shown. Overall effect is best if the colours alternate with each row.

For first row, start at 1 to 2 and work a group of three stitches, down the canvas, slanting each stitch from lower left to upper right. Then, at 3 to 4, work up the canvas, forming three stitches that slant from lower right to upper left. Continue to work across canvas, alternately working 1–2 and 3–4 stitch groups. At end of row, leave needle at back of canvas and turn canvas around.

Begin second row with a group of stitches slanted in a direction opposite to last group of preceding row. Start with a 1–2 or a 3–4 group, as needed; place all stitches of all groups to overlap groups of preceding row as shown. At end of row, turn canvas around.

Start third row with a group of stitches slanting the same way as the last group of row just completed. Start with a 3–4 or 1–2 group, as needed; position all stitches of all groups to 'nest' below those of the preceding row. At end of row, turn canvas around.

For fourth row, begin with a group slanting in the opposite direction to that of the last group of the row just completed (3–4 or 1–2, as required). Overlap all stitches in this row with those in the preceding row (see far right). At end of fourth row, turn canvas. Following the same four-row procedure just described, cover the entire canvas area with perspective stitches.

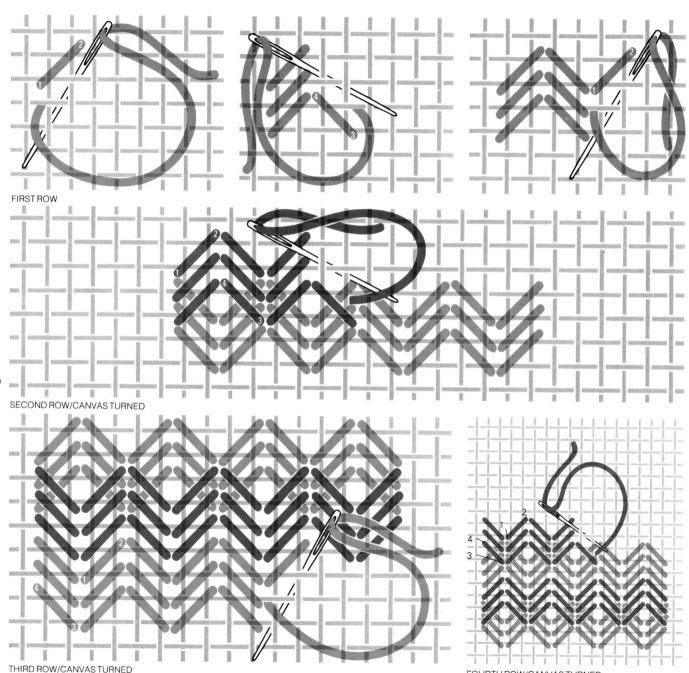

FIRST ROW

SECOND ROW/CANVAS TURNED

THIRD ROW/CANVAS TURNED

FOURTH ROW/CANVAS TURNED

Composite stitches

The stitches in this group are classified as composite stitches because each uses more than one of the other types of canvas stitches. For example, Algerian eye stitch (below) makes use of straight and diagonal stitches; triangle stitch (p. 49) contains straight and cross stitches. Except for the normal size Algerian eye stitch, all the composite stitches are large, and produce definite shapes rather than overall textures. As can occur with any large stitch, the thread may not completely cover the canvas mesh. To lessen the amount of canvas exposure, do not pull thread too tight while forming stitches.

Algerian eye stitch

Large Algerian eye stitch with backstitch

ALGERIAN EYE STITCHES

Algerian eye stitches form star-like units on the canvas. Each unit, whether normal size or the enlarged version, consists of eight small stitches worked around a common canvas hole. When selecting thread for this stitch, be sure that the thread will be able to pass through the common canvas hole eight times without distortion. If the selected thread does not adequately cover the canvas mesh, form backstitches around each unit as shown on left and below.

Algerian eye stitch. Begin at upper right and work rows alternately right to left, left to right. For each stitch unit, form eight small stitches, in a 1 to 8 sequence, around a centre hole, A. Bring needle out at a number, over one mesh or thread, then in at centre. When working rows right to left, work the eight stitches in a clockwise direction; when working rows from left to right, work them anticlockwise. Place the stitches of each new row below those of the preceding row.

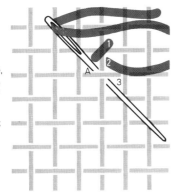 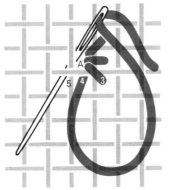  

Large Algerian eye stitch. This is a large version of Algerian eye stitch (above). Row formation and stitch unit construction are the same; the difference is that each of the eight stitches is now taken over two canvas threads or meshes. With a large Algerian eye stitch, it can be difficult to cover the canvas completely. To cover canvas threads still exposed, form backstitches (see p. 32) around the stitch units. Use either the same or a contrasting colour thread (contrasting colour used here).

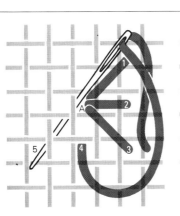 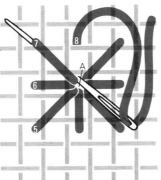 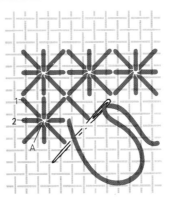 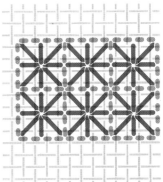

Canvas work stitches

Composite stitches

Ray stitch

Expanded ray stitch

RAY STITCHES

Each ray stitch and expanded ray stitch consists of several stitches that radiate from a common canvas hole. Ray stitch consists of seven stitches that form a square; an expanded ray stitch comprises 13 stitches that produce a rectangle. When selecting thread for either of these stitches, choose one that is thin enough so that the thread of the multiple stitches will fit through the common canvas hole without distortion. While working either of these stitches, do not pull the thread tight. For additional variety, alternate the colour with each unit or row of units.

Ray stitch. Begin at upper left and work rows alternately left to right, then right to left. Each ray stitch consists of seven stitches, fanned out around a common canvas hole, to cover a canvas area of three vertical by three horizontal canvas threads. Working anticlockwise and following a 1 to 7 sequence, begin each stitch at a number, end each in the common canvas hole, A. Fan each of the units as shown in the illustrations. At each row's end, reverse working direction; place new stitch units below those just done.

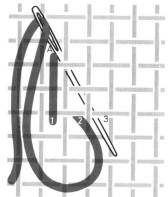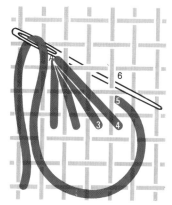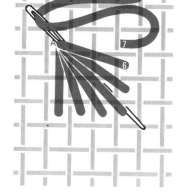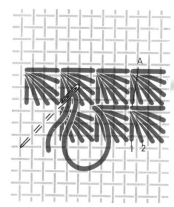

Expanded ray stitch. Start at upper left and work rows alternately left to right, then right to left. Each stitch unit consists of 13 stitches, fanned out around a common canvas hole, to cover six vertical by three horizontal canvas threads. Work stitches in a 1 to 13 sequence. For each stitch, bring needle out at a number, in at A. When working row from left to right, work anticlockwise; when working row from right to left, work clockwise. Place stitch units of each new row below those of preceding row.

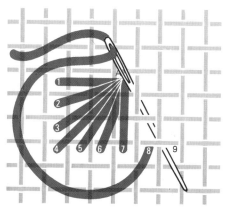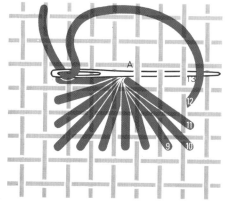

46

Diamond eyelet stitch

Diamond eyelet stitch with backstitch

DIAMOND EYELET STITCH

Diamond eyelet stitch is a pretty but large stitch. In fact, one diamond eyelet stitch can be used alone as a detail in a canvas work design. Each unit is composed of 16 stitches, all emanating from one centre canvas hole. Select thread weight carefully so that it will pass through the same canvas hole 16 times with no distortion. If the stitches do not adequately cover the canvas threads, backstitches can be worked over them (see left and below). Because of its long stitches, the diamond eyelet stitch is not recommended for items that will be subject to hard wear.

Diamond eyelet stitch. Begin at upper left and work rows alternately left to right, then right to left. Each diamond eyelet stitch consists of 16 stitches that form a diamond-shaped unit over eight vertical by eight horizontal canvas threads. Start first stitch, 1, in the fifth canvas hole from the corner. Then, working clockwise, form the other stitches, 2 to 16, as shown. Begin each stitch at a number; end each in the centre canvas hole, A. Start each new stitch unit in the eighth canvas hole from the start (1) of the unit just completed.

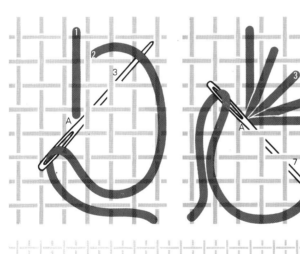

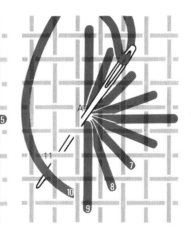

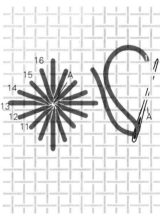

With each new row, reverse the working direction. Place new stitch units so that the first stitch, 1, shares a canvas hole with the horizontal stitches of the units in the preceding row. If desired, add backstitches (see p. 32) to cover the exposed canvas threads between the stitch units. Use the same or a contrasting colour.

Canvas work stitches

Composite stitches

Leaf stitch

Leaf stitch with backstitch

LEAF STITCH

Leaf stitch is another relatively large stitch that can be used alone or in groups. Each leaf stitch uses 11 stitches to form a leaf shape. Five stitches are fanned to form the top of the leaf shape and there are three stitches, in a vertical row, on each side of the unit. If you want to make the leaf shape longer, increase equally the number of stitches in each vertical (side) row; the five stitches at the top remain the same. To give the leaf shape some additional detail, work backstitches in centre of each unit; use the same or a contrasting thread.

Leaf stitch. Start in upper left corner (at 1); work rows alternately left to right, then right to left. Each leaf stitch unit shown here consists of 11 stitches – three side stitches; five fanned out to form the top of the leaf; then three stitches for the second side. (Units can be made longer by working more but equal numbers of stitches on each side.) Work side stitches first, 1 to 6, then top stitches, 7 to 16, then other side stitches, 17 to 22. For each stitch, bring needle out at an odd number, in at an even number. When working rows from left to right, work stitches clockwise; when working right to left, work anticlockwise. Begin each new unit in the sixth canvas hole from the start (1) of the unit just completed.

With each new row, reverse direction for working rows and units. Position new units so their top parts are nested as shown along the lower edges of the units in the preceding row. For extra detail, backstitches (see p. 32) can be formed up or down the centre of each leaf stitch unit. Colour of thread for the backstitches can be the same as or a contrast to the colour used for leaf stitches.

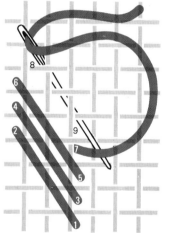

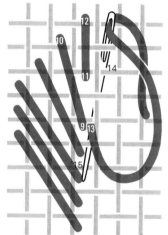

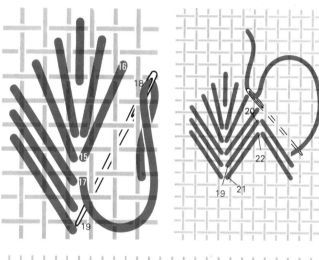

Triangle stitch (one colour of thread used)

Triangle stitch (two colours of thread used)

TRIANGLE STITCH

Triangle stitch, which is square in its overall shape, is made up of four triangular shapes placed point to point. A large cross stitch in each corner completes the unit and squares off its shape. The patterns produced by triangle stitches can be very interesting. When all the stitches are worked in the same colour, the basic square shape of a unit will sometimes appear to go back, while neighbouring groups of triangles come forward to form secondary patterns. The use of a second colour increases the range of possible patterns.

Triangle stitch. Each stitch unit (see the fourth drawing below) consists of four triangles placed point to point to produce straight outer edges. Cross stitches at corners square off and complete unit. Start first row at upper left; work rows alternately left to right, then right to left.

For each inner triangular unit, work seven stitches, 1 to 14 as shown, bringing needle out at an odd number, in at an even number. Stitch top triangular unit first; work all units and stitches in an anticlockwise direction. Place triangles as shown, bringing needle out of the same canvas hole for each of the four 7's. Although not shown, canvas can be turned a quarter to work each triangle.

Complete triangle stitch unit by working a large cross stitch (see p. 33), over two by two canvas meshes, in each of the four corners. Start in upper right corner and work cross stitches as shown, A to D. (Note: working order of first cross stitch is different from other three.) Begin next triangle stitch in tenth canvas hole from start of stitch unit just done. With each new row, reverse direction for working row. Place new stitch units below those just completed.

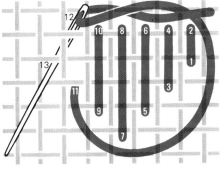

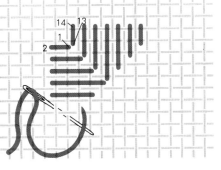

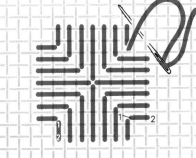

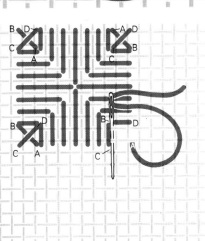

Canvas work stitches

Composite stitches

Brighton stitch (one colour of thread used)

Brighton stitch (two colours of thread used)

BRIGHTON STITCH

Brighton stitch is produced by rows of diagonal stitches; these are worked in blocks, and the slant of the stitches alternates from block to block. Each new row of stitches is a mirror image of the row above; sets of rows form a pattern of diamond shapes. An upright cross stitch in the centre of each diamond completes the Brighton unit. The upright cross stitches can be worked in the same or a contrasting colour, as shown in the samples on the left.

Brighton stitch. Rows consist of blocks of diagonal stitches. Each block has five stitches; the slant alternates with each block. Sets of rows form diamond-shaped units. An upright cross stitch is worked in centre of each diamond.

Start at upper left; work all rows from left to right. Begin first row with a block of five stitches that slant from lower left to upper right, 1 to 10. Then work the next block of five stitches, slanting them from lower right to upper left, 11 to 20. Continue to work across the canvas, alternately forming 1–10 and 11–20 stitch blocks. At end of each row, leave needle at back of canvas and turn canvas around.

Begin each new row with a block of stitches that slant in a direction opposite to the slant of the last block in the row just completed. Start with either a 1–10 or an 11–20 block as required.

Cover entire canvas area with rows of stitches. Then, form an upright cross stitch in the centre of each diamond, A to D, as explained on p. 36.

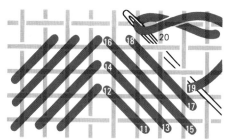

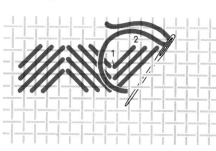

FIRST ROW

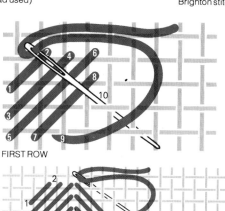

SECOND ROW/CANVAS TURNED

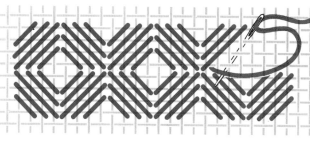

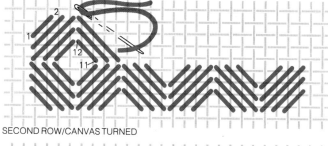

THIRD ROW/CANVAS TURNED

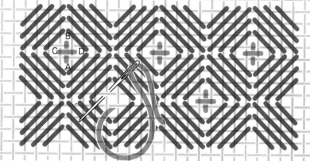

Pile stitches

There are only three stitches in this canvas work stitch group. They are all alike in that each produces a texture that extends out from the surface of the can-vas. This extended surface, referred to as a pile, is produced by the loops of thread formed with the stitches. These loops may remain in their uncut form or they can be cut. The loop-cutting tech-nique is explained on the next page with the velvet stitch; it can be used, how-ever, for any of the three stitches in this group. Pile stitches are most commonly used for rugs, but they are suitable for any type of canvas work item that calls for a pile surface.

RYA (OR GHIORDES KNOT) STITCH/ VELVET STITCH/SURREY STITCH

Though these three stitches are alike in forming a pile surface, they differ in individual construction. Additional dif-ferences, due to different positioning, can occur with each of the three. These stem from the type of canvas (single, rug or double) the stitch is being worked on, and are explained as they arise. For more about canvases, see p. 8.

Rya stitch

Velvet stitch

Surrey stitch

Rya stitch (on single or rug canvas). Begin at lower left; work all rows left to right. For first stitch of each row, hold thread end on right side of canvas. Work each Rya stitch as follows: pass needle under one vertical canvas thread, 1 to 2, and pull thread through. Curve excess thread up, pass needle under next vertical thread, 3 to 4; pull thread through. Form loop of desired length; hold in place while forming next and each successive Rya stitch. Work stitches of new row above row just done. If desired, cut loops (see next page).

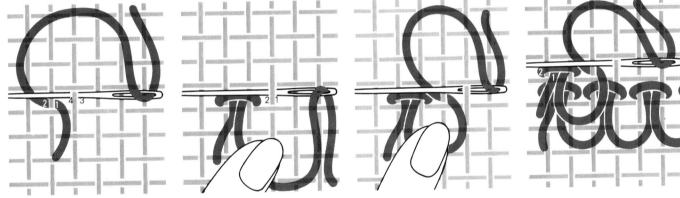

Rya stitch (on double canvas). Stitch and row construction are same as above, but the position of the stitch can vary. When using double canvas, each Rya stitch can be formed above two canvas meshes, like stitches above, or one mesh, as shown on the right. To work a Rya stitch above one mesh of double canvas, spread double set of vertical threads and treat as single threads while forming the stitch. Pass needle under one thread, 1 to 2, then under the next thread, 3 to 4.

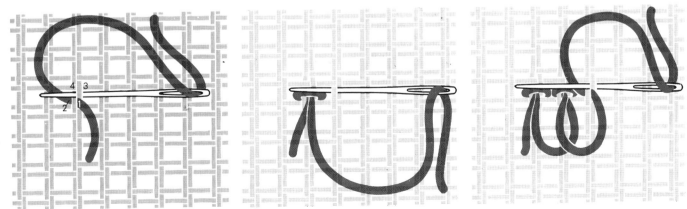

Canvas work stitches

Pile stitches

Velvet stitch (on single or rug canvas). Begin at lower left; work rows left to right. Work each velvet stitch as follows: bring needle out at 1, up over two canvas meshes, in at 2, then out at 3 (same hole as 1). Form a loop of desired length; hold in place. Insert needle at 4 (same hole as 2), under two horizontal threads (or two sets of threads if using rug canvas), and out at 5 with point of needle under loop. Then pass needle back over two meshes and in at 6. Begin next stitch in same canvas hole as the 5 of the stitch just done.

Work velvet stitches across the canvas, placing them next to each other. For each new row, begin at the left; place new stitches above those in the row just done. When all rows are completed, the loops can be cut, if so desired.

To cut the loops, open scissors and slide blade through a few loops (illustration on the far right). Cut the loops while slightly tugging on them with the scissors blade. Proceed to the next group of loops and cut them in the same manner.

Velvet stitch (on double canvas). Both row and stitch formation are the same as above. The only difference is another stitch-position possibility permitted by the double-mesh canvas. Each velvet stitch can be worked over two meshes, as on single canvas above; or over only one mesh, as on the right, following this procedure: bring needle out at 1, over one double mesh, in at 2; out at 3, over the same mesh, and in at 4. Then under a set of horizontal threads, and out at 5; back over the double mesh, and in at 6.

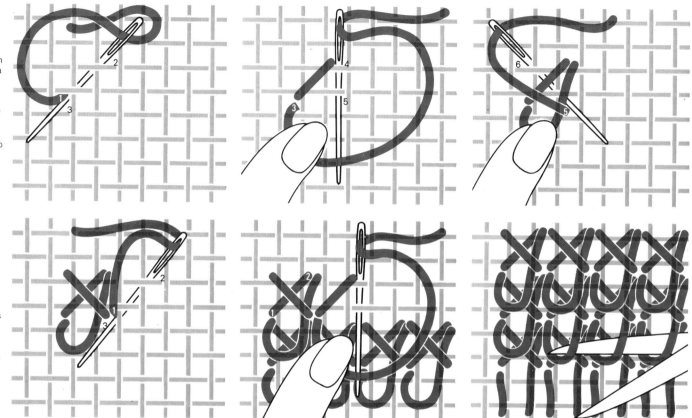

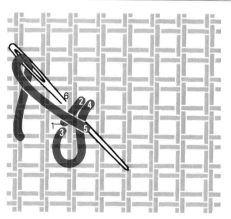

Surrey stitch (on single or rug canvas). Start at lower left; work all rows left to right. For first stitch of each row, hold thread end on right side of canvas. Work each Surrey stitch as follows: insert needle at 1, pass under two horizontal threads (two sets of threads if using rug canvas), bring out at 2. Pull excess yarn through and curve up as in the second illustration. Bring needle over two meshes, in at 3, under two vertical threads, then out at 4 with point of needle over excess curved thread. Pull thread through. Form a loop of desired length; hold in place while forming the next and each successive Surrey stitch. For each new stitch, start in the same canvas hole as the 3 of stitch just done; make sure that when needle is brought out at 2, its point passes over the loop of thread (far right).

With each new row, start again at the left and place the new stitches above those in the row just done. When all rows are finished, the loops may be cut if so desired. Cutting of loops is explained on opposite page.

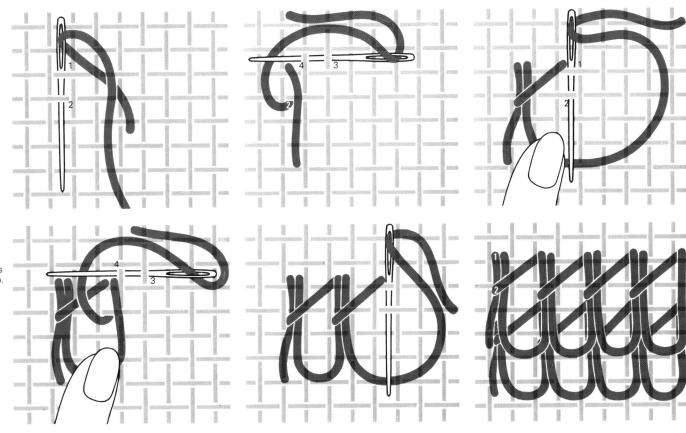

Surrey stitch (on double canvas). Row and stitch formation are the same as above. The only difference that can occur is in the placing of stitches. With double canvas, each Surrey stitch can be done over two meshes, as above, or over only one mesh, as are the stitches on the right. When working a Surrey stitch over only one mesh of double canvas, consider the pairs of threads as single units and work stitch as shown, 1 to 2, then 3 to 4.

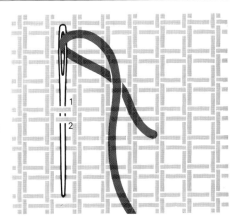
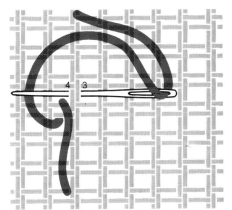
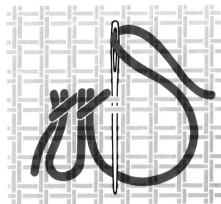

Canvas work stitches

Additional stitching techniques

The technique discussed below, **multi-colour** stitching, is a process of forming a colour pattern while working a canvas work stitch pattern. The colour designs can be formed by changing the thread colour with each row or by placing the various colours within the same row. The technique at the top of the opposite page, **filling-in stitches,** concerns the formation of partial stitch patterns along the edge of an area. The last technique, **left-handed** stitching, is at the bottom of the facing page. It explains how the instructions and illustrations given for stitches in this section can be adapted by a left-handed person.

MULTI-COLOUR STITCHING

The use of more than one thread colour to work an area of stitches actually produces two patterns. One is the pattern created by the stitch itself, the other results from the arrangement of the various colours. There are two ways of introducing different thread colours: row by row (Method 1) or within a row (Method 2). With both methods, the individual stitches are formed in their usual way, but the procedure for working the rows of stitches is altered.

In **Method 1,** the new thread colour is introduced with each row of stitches and the rows are worked in row-units, with each unit consisting of as many rows as there are colours. When rows are being worked normally, the working direction is reversed or the canvas is turned at the end of each row. When you are working with row-units, this change occurs with the first row of each new unit. With Method 1, each colour is threaded into a separate needle. If there is excess thread at the end of a row, it is brought up to the right side of the canvas and secured away from the working area. When you are ready to work a new row in that colour, the excess thread is brought to the wrong side of the canvas to the point where the new row begins.

Method 2 places the different colours within a row of stitches. It works best when only two thread colours are used for a stitch pattern that contains two stitch types. One such pattern is the double stitch, in which oblong cross stitches alternate with one-mesh cross stitches. First, all the rows of one stitch type and colour are worked, leaving spaces for the other stitch type. Then, the other stitch type is worked in the spaces left, with the second colour.

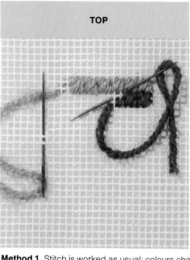

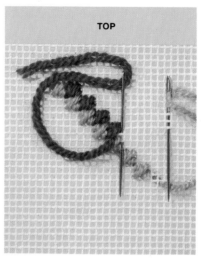

Method 1. Stitch is worked as usual; colours change with each new row; rows are worked in units. The examples (both mosaic stitches) are worked in two colours so that two rows constitute a unit. Both rows in left sample are worked right to left; both in right sample are worked diagonally down.

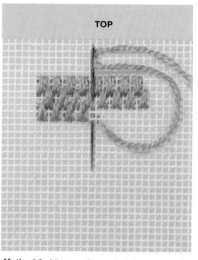

Method 2. All rows of one stitch type are worked as usual, leaving spaces for the second. Base stitches here are oblong cross stitches.

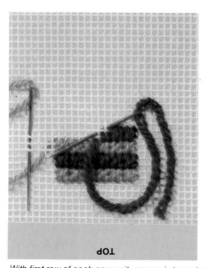

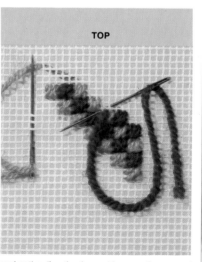

With first row of each new unit, canvas is turned around or the direction for working rows is reversed. Which it is depends on the way the rows of the stitch are usually done. Left sample was turned to work new unit; working direction was reversed in right sample.

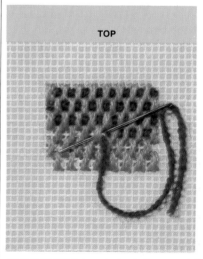

Work next stitch type and colour in the spaces left by first stitches. One-mesh cross stitches here complete the double stitch pattern.

FILLING-IN STITCHES

The photographs below (details of the ornamental stitch barn shown on p. 7) illustrate filling-in stitches in use.

Filling-in stitches are partial stitch patterns worked along the edge of a design area. They cover the open spans of canvas that are too small to hold full stitches of the pattern in that area. Their purpose is to maintain the effect of the area's stitch pattern (and colour pattern) all the way out to its edges. They are formed along with the full stitches, and the length of each filling-in stitch is equal to the span of canvas left between the edge and a full-size stitch.

LEFT-HANDED STITCHING

All of the stitches in this section are illustrated and explained for the use of a right-handed person. If you are left-handed, these illustrations and explanations can be adapted for your use.

To begin with, read and familiarise yourself with the way the stitch is done by a right-handed person. Then, when you are ready to work, turn the book and your canvas upside-down. Begin working your stitches in the same corner that now appears in the upside-down illustration, and work the row in the direction that it shows. Read the upside-down numbers in numerical order and follow that sequence for forming the stitch. If the instructions say to turn the canvas or reverse the working direction with each row of stitches, do so. If they indicate that all the rows are to be worked in one direction, work all your rows in the one direction that now appears in the upside-down illustration. Shown on the right are three canvas work stitches. The top three illustrations show the stitches in the right-handed working order. The lower three show these same illustrations but turned to an upside-down position for left-handed use.

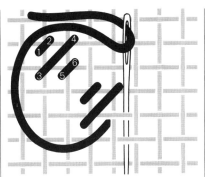

Tent stitches, done horizontally. Work from right to left; turn canvas with each row.

Mosaic stitches, done diagonally. Work first row down; reverse direction with each row.

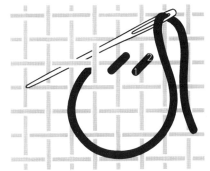

Fern stitches. Start at upper left and work all rows down the canvas.

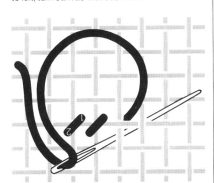

If left-handed, turn canvas upside-down. Work from left to right; turn canvas with each row.

If left-handed, turn canvas upside-down. Work first row up; reverse direction with each row.

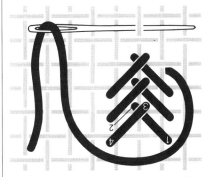

If left-handed, turn canvas, start in lower right corner and work all rows up the canvas.

Designing and making canvas work

Design elements

The design used for any canvas work is affected by several elements. With a kit, these elements have already been correlated so that all you have to do is stitch the design according to the instructions. When you are creating your own design, you must be aware of many things. First, you should know about the three different appearances that canvas work stitches can achieve (see p. 7). Also important is a basic knowledge of the materials (pp. 8–9), and the stitches (pp. 12–55) used in canvas work. The more you know about these, the easier it will be for you to combine the design elements discussed on these two pages. (The elements described here do not apply to the design of Florentine embroidery, however; for more detailed information about Florentine work, see p. 67).

The most important element is the **design** itself. It should complement and be in proportion to the size and shape of the finished item. A design can consist of one motif on a plain background, or it can be a composition that fills the entire space. (Many compositions are repeats of a single motif, see pp. 64–65.) Most canvas work designs are asymmetrical, that is, their components are different from area to area (barn design on p. 7 is asymmetrical). Some canvas work designs are symmetrical in that their parts (halves or quarters) are mirror-images of each other (pp. 62–63). If you are good at drawing, you can create a design. If you are not, trace the design from an existing source, such as a book, a plate or a piece of fabric. While you are still working out the design, it is best to keep your drawing to a manageable size. It can then be enlarged or reduced later, when you are ready to transfer it to canvas.

The amount of detail in the design must also be considered; this determines the **gauge of canvas** you should use. A design with simple shapes or large masses of colour can be carried out on a large-gauge canvas (under 10). A simple shape with moderate curves and some detail and colour shadings can be done on medium-gauge canvas (from 10 to 14). Whether simple or complex, a design with strong curves, small details and considerable shading will require a fine-gauge (16 to 20). An extremely delicate or small design could require a canvas even finer (over 20 gauge). The gauge of your canvas will affect the amount of time you spend stitching and the durability of the finished item. In general, the finer the gauge, the more time spent in stitching, but the more durable the final result. If you do not want to use the recommended gauge, you can either select another design better suited to the canvas you prefer, or adapt the design you have to the limita-tions of that canvas gauge. For example, a very fine design can be re-drawn with larger details and less definite curves so that it will be suitable to a medium-gauge canvas.

How much detail your stitched design has will depend on the size and texture of the **stitches** you select. There are basically only two stitch categories, tent stitches and ornamental stitches. Tent stitches are the smallest of the canvas work stitches, and so are best for translating drawn lines or details. If you plan to use tent stitches, your design can be as detailed as the intended canvas gauge will allow. The ornamental stitches (except for the one-mesh cross stitch) are larger than tent stitches and therefore less suitable for expressing drawn lines and small details. The beauty of the ornamental stitches, however, is in the texture that each produces, and the way that these textures interpret design motifs. When drawing a design for ornamental stitches, keep the lines simple and eliminate small details. How simplified these should be depends on the area of a particular stitch. Some of the smaller ornamental stitches are capable of creating simple colour shadings. The samples and illustrations in the stitch section will help you to determine the space requirements of particular stitches. Remember also that you can mix tent and ornamental stitches in the

Drawing of a leaf

Tent stitches on 18-gauge canvas

Tent stitches on 12-gauge canvas

same design. When drawing any design, place the lines and details as best you can; they can be refined further as you work the stitches on to the canvas. If you want to be very accurate in your placing, the design can be charted (see p. 66). If your design is symmetrical or a multiple repeat, it should be charted.

Shown below is a leaf shape stitched on to four different gauges of canvas. The first three are worked with tent stitches, the fourth with Byzantine stitch, an ornamental stitch. All four were based on the same drawing, and each spans the same area of canvas. The first tent-stitch leaf is on an 18-gauge canvas, the second on a 12-gauge, the third on a 7-gauge; the ornamental-stitch leaf is on a 10-gauge canvas. Notice how the leaf shape becomes less detailed and its lines simpler as the gauge and the stitches grow larger. For another example of the change that stitches can make in design lines and areas, compare the differences in the two stitched barns that are shown on p. 7. Both samples were based on the same drawing of a barn scene.

With any canvas work stitch, a part of the textural effect comes from the way light strikes the thread on the canvas. If you alter the direction the thread (stitch) takes on the canvas, you also change the way the light hits the thread. Changing the direction of a stitch is a simple work-ing procedure, explained on the far right. This technique will affect any stitch except those, like the diamond eyelet, in which the thread is laid in all directions. It will also change the direction of some stitch patterns. For example, when fern stitch is worked normally (p. 41), it produces a pattern of up-and-down stripes. When the fern stitch is worked with the method explained on the right, the stripes go across the canvas.

The type of thread used to work a stitch will also affect its texture. Loosely twisted types, such as Persian wool, produce a softer surface than do those that are more tightly twisted, such as tapestry wool. Those that are inherently shiny, such as pearl cottons and the metallic threads, will add a bit of sparkle to the stitches. When deciding on the type of thread to use, also consider its durability. Threads that are made of wool, cotton or acrylic are stronger than those made of rayon or synthetic metal. Choose threads which are suitable for your design and for its eventual use.

When selecting the **colours** for your design, choose a scheme that you like and that will enhance the design. After you have selected your colours, colour in the drawing so that you can see how they look together. When you go to shop for threads, use the colours in the drawing as a general guide.

Changing the direction of a stitch

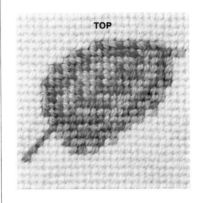

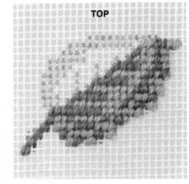

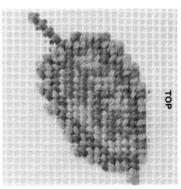

To change the direction of a stitch or of its pattern on the canvas, work the stitch as usual, but hold the canvas so that its top edge is at the side. If the canvas needs to be turned around to work each new row of stitches, do so, but turn it so that the top edge alternates from right to left sides. The finished leaf on the left shows tent stitches slanting in opposite directions. The first illustration below shows the canvas with its top edge in the normal position to produce tent stitches with a normal slant (for the lower half of leaf). The second shows the canvas with its top at the side to produce tent stitches with the opposing slant (for the upper half of leaf). To avoid confusion while using this technique, label the top edge of the canvas.

Tent stitches on 7-gauge canvas

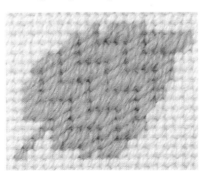

Byzantine stitch on 10-gauge canvas

Selecting working techniques

There are many different working techniques in canvas work; it is up to you to select the ones you will need to use. Many of the techniques apply to the way the design is transferred to the canvas. These can be divided into methods for transferring uncharted designs (pp. 58–59) and charted designs (pp. 60–65). Techniques applying to Florentine work, another class of charted designs, begin on p. 67. Read all of these pages and choose the technique recommended for the type of design you are using. Before any design can be transferred to the canvas, the canvas must be prepared (p. 58). General working techniques that can be used with any type of design are described on the last few instructional pages of this book. The information on estimating thread amounts enables you to calculate the quantities of threads needed to stitch any design, especially one that you designed yourself. The other techniques – setting canvas into a frame, removing stitches, repairing canvas and blocking – will help you to make your canvas work as near perfect as possible.

Designing and making canvas work

Basic preparations

To begin canvas work, you must first prepare a piece of canvas large enough to receive the design. 'Large enough' means the finished size of the design plus a margin of at least 5 cm along each edge. When you are working with an uncharted design, finished size equals the dimensions of the drawing you will follow. When a design is charted, finished size depends upon the number of canvas threads called for by the chart in relation to the threads per centimetre in the canvas. If the canvas is too narrow, lengths can be joined to get the necessary width (centre right). Make a pattern of the prepared canvas (far right); it will be needed when it is time to block the worked canvas.

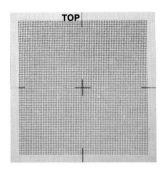

Basic preparation of canvas. Cut canvas to finished size of design plus a margin (5 cm minimum) along each edge. Bind edges with tape; label top edge. Mark vertical and horizontal centres. If centres are on threads, mark at middle of canvas and on each side as above. If centres are between threads, tack with wool (see p. 59).

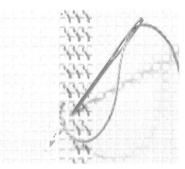

To join lengths of canvas to produce necessary width. Cut two pieces to required length. Place side by side and cut off neighbouring selvedges. Overlap cut edges by 3 to 4 vertical threads and match all threads and meshes. Using strong thread, work down each row of matched threads, oversewing around every other matched mesh.

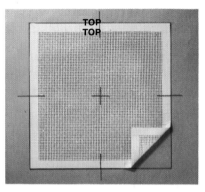

To make a pattern of prepared canvas. Place canvas on a piece of brown paper and trace its outlines. Indicate top edge on paper and mark centre of each edge. Keep pattern; it will be needed to block the worked canvas.

Placing the design on canvas/Method 1

This design transfer method places both the shapes and the colours of the design on to the canvas. The stitches are then worked right over the painted design. This method is recommended for use with any uncharted design, especially one that uses tent stitches only. Before a design of this type can be transferred, both the drawing and the finished size of the canvas must be equal to the finished size of the item for which the canvas work is being done. To transfer the design to the canvas, use only waterproof colouring pens or paints. If you are not absolutely sure about any pen, do not use it; colours that are not waterproof are likely to run while the worked canvas is being blocked. Use the painted canvas as a guide to calculate the amount of thread that will be needed.

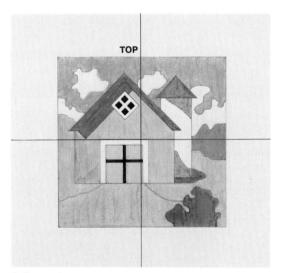

1. Draw a line down and another line across the centre of the drawing. If necessary, label top edge and establish outer lines of design area. Prepare canvas as explained at top of page.

2. Place prepared canvas over drawing; match its centre lines to those in drawing. Pin layers together and paint design on to canvas. Copy shapes in drawing; use matching or similar colours.

3. When canvas is dry, work stitches right over the design. Work an area or a colour at a time. Place stitches at the edges of an area as close as you can to its painted edges.

Placing the design on canvas/Method 2

This method of transfer puts the lines of a design, but not its colours, on the canvas. It is recommended for use with any uncharted design, particularly one calling for some ornamental stitches.

Both the canvas and the drawing of the design are prepared as for Method 1; if ornamental stitches are being used, the name of the stitch is noted in appropriate areas on the drawing. To transfer the lines to the canvas, use markers that are waterproof and neutral in colour. As you work an ornamental stitch area, modify the size or shape of the area to conform to the space needs of the selected stitch. If you would prefer to check and perhaps adjust an ornamental stitch area before transferring its lines to the canvas, chart the area and the stitch as explained at the bottom of this page.

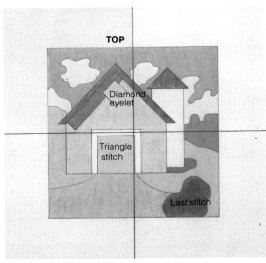

1. Draw a horizontal and a vertical line through centre of drawing. Label each ornamental stitch area with its name. Prepare the canvas as explained at the top of the preceding page.

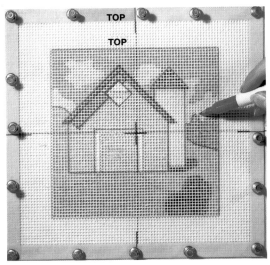

2. Place canvas on top of drawing and match centre markings. Pin layers together and transfer lines of design to canvas. To chart an area before transferring its lines, see below.

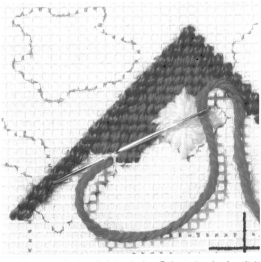

3. When canvas is dry, stitch the design. Refer to drawing for stitch and colour placing. When you work ornamental stitches, use filling-in stitches to fill gaps, or alter area to fit stitch.

TO CHART AN AREA

1. With the design area in position under the canvas, count out, at its widest points, the number of canvas threads that the area spans across and up and down. The area being checked is the bush in the lower right corner of the design. Leaf stitches are planned.

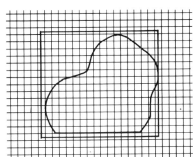

2. On a piece of graph paper (any gauge), count out these same totals in graphed lines and draw a box to enclose them. Then, referring to the area under the canvas, sketch shape on graph paper, crossing its lines in same way as lines cross canvas threads.

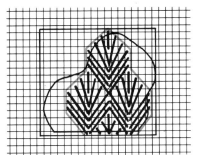

3. Sketch stitch pattern in outlined area. For help, see illustration in stitch section. If stitches nearly fill area, gaps can be filled with filling-in stitches. If they cover too much or too little, adjust lines to fit stitch (above) or use a stitch better suited to the area.

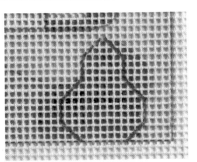

4. Referring to the graph paper, transfer the area's outline (with changes, if any) to the canvas. Make sure that the lines cross the canvas threads the same way they cross the graph paper lines. When stitching this area, refer to its chart for guidance in placing the stitches.

Designing and making canvas work

Understanding charts

Some canvas work designs are presented in chart form, that is, the position of each stitch in the design is recorded on graph paper. Graph paper is used for charting because it is structurally similar to canvas. Its vertical and horizontal lines correspond to the canvas threads; the squares and intersections made by the crossing lines are like the holes and meshes of the canvas. Both come in several gauges, related to the number of sub-divisions (squares with graph paper; threads with canvas) to the centimetre. There are two ways to make use of these similarities, and each produces a different type of chart.

With a **box chart,** the squares on the graph paper represent the threads and/or meshes of the canvas. For a tent stitch, one square means one mesh. With straight or ornamental stitches, a square means one thread or mesh of the stitch's total span. The total span is represented by the requisite number of squares, heavily outlined. For example, a straight Gobelin stitch, four threads long, is represented by an outlined row of four squares. A large Algerian eye stitch, which spans four by four meshes, is represented by a group of four by four squares with a heavy outline.

Line charts are an exact duplication of how the stitches will be laid over the canvas threads and meshes. A tent stitch is a slanted line over one intersection of a pair of lines. A straight Gobelin stitch, four threads long, is a straight line over four lines. A large Algerian eye stitch is represented by eight lines drawn over a group of intersections and lines and converging in a centre square.

In either type of chart, the colour of the stitch is indicated with actual colours or with symbols in black and shades of grey. With a box chart, the square is filled with either the colour or the symbol. With a line chart, the indications are incorporated in the drawn line. If the chart is in colours, the line is drawn in the colour. If symbols are being used, the symbol is made a part of the drawn line. Since there is no standardisation of the character and meaning of symbols, they will differ from chart to chart. Sometimes the colour symbols also indicate a type of thread. With other charts, letters or numbers represent colours, stitches or threads.

An integral companion to a chart is a listing, or key, that translates the meanings of the symbols in the chart. There can be one or more keys. In addition to a key, some charted designs also include a simplified (schematic) line drawing to explain some aspect of the design that is not covered by the chart or key. For several typical examples of symbols and keys used with box and line charts, refer to the symbol chart below.

In order to work a charted design on canvas, you will need a piece of canvas that contains at least the total number of threads needed to stitch the entire design. This thread number is based on the number of threads the chart calls for across and up and down, and the number of times the chart must be followed to produce the complete design. If the chart depicts a *full design* (see next page), it will be followed only once, and the total number of threads needed is just the amount contained in the chart. If it is a *partial design chart*, of which there are several types, it must be followed more than once to produce the total design, and the total thread requirements will therefore be a multiple of the number called for by the chart (see pp. 62–65).

After total thread requirements have been calculated, cut and prepare canvas. Be sure to add a minimum 5 cm margin along each edge before cutting the canvas. The measurements of the prepared canvas will of course vary according to the gauge of the canvas, since it is by the number of threads per centimetre that canvas gauges differ.

TYPES OF CHARTING SYMBOLS

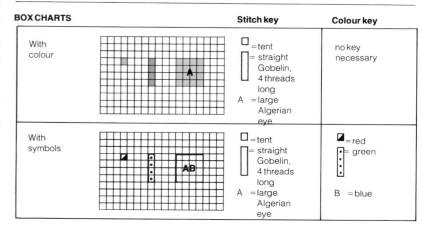

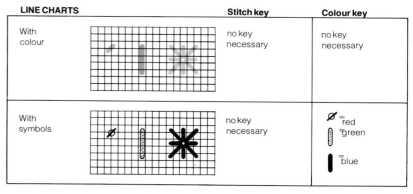

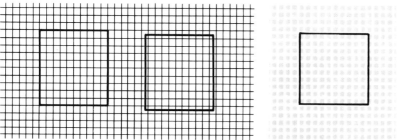

To calculate canvas thread requirements of a charted design, first count the threads across and up and down that the chart calls for. Then match these numbers with same number of canvas threads across and up and down. First chart area above represents 10 by 10 threads on a box chart; the second represents 10 by 10 threads on a line chart. Area of canvas on the right has 10 by 10 threads.

Full design charts

A full design chart is one in which all areas of the total design are represented. A partial design chart (pp. 62–65) lays out only one area; this one area, repeated, makes up the total design. The need for a full charting comes from the asymmetrical structure of a design, that is, from all of its areas being different. When you are using a full chart, the number of canvas threads necessary to stitch the design is the same as the number of threads in the chart. With a kit or chart that does not supply the canvas, you will need to determine the span of canvas that is required by the design. To do this, first determine whether the chart is a box or a line chart, and then notice how each represents threads (see preceding page) so that you will understand how to interpret yours. Once this is understood, count the threads across and up and down called for by the chart. Then calculate the quantity of canvas that will be needed to supply these same numbers of threads across and up and down, and add to this a minimum 5 cm margin along each of the edges. The overall dimensions of the canvas will vary according to its gauge; the finer the gauge being used, the smaller the finished size will be. The gauge of canvas should also be suitable to the design (see pp. 56–57) as well as to the size of the item it is intended for. If the chosen gauge of canvas will produce too small or too large a finished size, you have several options. You could change to a different gauge of canvas that would give you a more suitable finished size. If the design has a background area, it can be enlarged or reduced by using more or fewer stitches in the background. If a design needs enlarging and has no background area, one can be added if this would be appropriate to the design's character. There is no way to reduce such a design except to change the canvas gauge.

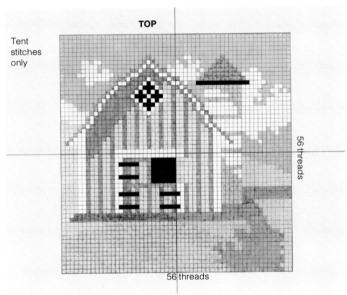

Tent stitches only

TOP

56 threads

56 threads

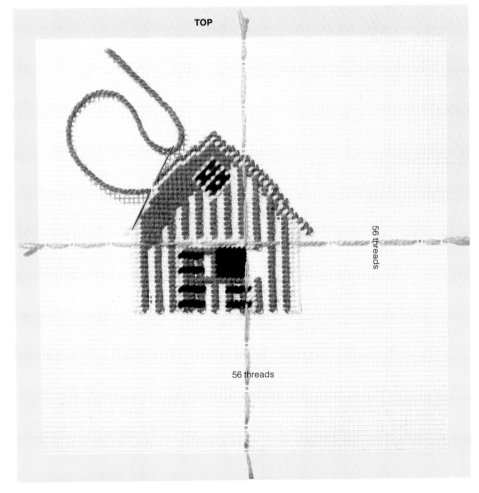

TOP

56 threads

56 threads

1. First locate and then draw horizontal and vertical centre lines on the chart. If necessary, also label the top edge of the charted design. Count the number of threads across and up and down that are called for by the chart.

2. Prepare canvas for work. Calculate its measurements to be sure it contains the same number of threads across and up and down as called for by the chart. To this add a margin (minimum 5 cm) along each edge. Cut canvas to these overall measurements. Bind the edges with tape and label the top edge. Locate and mark the vertical and horizontal centres of the canvas. If the chart calls for an uneven number of threads, the centre falls on a thread, as shown on p. 164. If the chart involves an even number of threads, the centre is between threads and is marked with tackings in wool (see right). Use a pale colour for tackings; stitch over or remove them as you work.

3. Stitch the design on the canvas. Refer to chart (and to keys, if necessary) for the stitch type, placing and colour. Use the centre markings on chart and canvas as reference points for locating areas. Work design from the centre out, an area or colour at a time. If there is a background, work this part last.

Designing and making canvas work

Partial design charts

A partial design chart presents only a portion of the total design. The reason for the partial representation is that the total design consists of repeats of that portion. There are several types of partial design charts. One type is used to form a multiple-repeat design (p.64); another is the row chart used to work Florentine embroidery (p. 67). The two partial design charts that are discussed here are half-charts and quarter-charts; it is these that are used to form symmetrical designs.

A symmetrical design consists of two or four repeats that meet and mirror each other at the design's centre. If there are two repeats, one on each side of a centre line, the design has two-way symmetry. A half-chart, followed twice, will produce a two-way symmetrical design. If the parts are on each side of a horizontal centre line, as in the fish design on the right, the chart used is a **horizontal half-chart**. If they are on each side of a vertical centre line, as is the butterfly shown below, the chart used is a **vertical half-chart**. When there are four units that are arranged around horizontal and vertical centre lines, the design has a four-way symmetry (see the tile design on the opposite page). A **quarter-chart**, followed four times, will produce a four-way symmetrical design.

The total number of canvas threads required to work a symmetrical design is a multiple of the number called for by the chart. These calculations are explained with the individual charts. When working the half or quarter represented by the chart, place its areas in the same positions as shown on the chart. When working the non-charted halves or quarters, place their areas so they mirror the comparable areas on the other side of the centre. It is not necessary to start and stop stitching at the centre lines. An exception to this: when you are alternating the direction of the stitches in each repeat (see opposite).

Horizontal half-charts

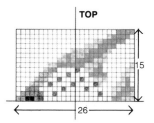

1. Label top of chart. Draw a line down the vertical centre of the design, another line across its horizontal centre. The total number of canvas threads required for the entire design is the *same* as the number of threads that the chart calls for across the design but *double* the number of threads indicated on the chart from the horizontal centre to the design's edge. Prepare canvas for work. Label its top edge and mark its vertical and horizontal centres as well (p. 61).

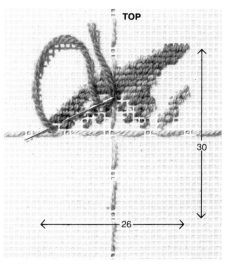

2. Work the top half of the design on canvas. Use the centre markings on the chart to locate areas and work them in exactly the same positions on the canvas, using its centre markings as guides.

3. To work the lower half, use the chart to locate areas; place them on the canvas in the same relation to the vertical centre of the canvas but in the reverse position in relation to its horizontal centre.

Vertical half-charts

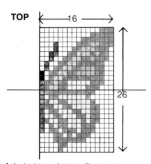

1. Label top of chart. Draw a line across the horizontal centre of design, another line down its vertical centre. Total number of threads needed for the entire design *equals* the number of threads the chart calls for from top to bottom of the design but *is double* the number from the design's vertical centre to its edge. Prepare canvas. Label its top edge and mark its vertical and horizontal centres (p. 61).

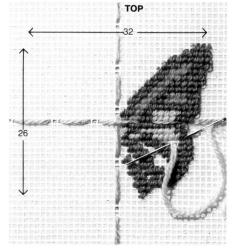

2. Work the right half of the design on the canvas. Use the centre markings on the chart to locate areas and place these areas in the same positions on the canvas, using its centre lines as guides.

3. To work the left half, use the chart to locate areas. Place the areas on the canvas in the same relation to the horizontal centre but in the reverse relation to the vertical centre.

Quarter-charts

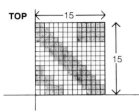

TOP ← 15 → 15

1. Label top of chart. Draw a line down the vertical centre of the design, another line across its horizontal centre. The total number of canvas threads necessary for the entire design is *double* the number of threads that the chart calls for from the vertical centre to the edge and from the horizontal centre to the edge. Prepare the canvas. Label its top edge; mark its vertical and horizontal centres (p. 61). To work the upper quarters, hold chart with its top edge up and use it to locate areas.

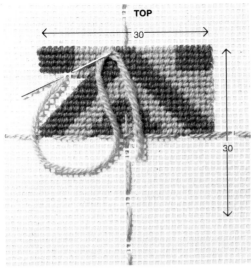

TOP ← 30 → 30

2. Place areas in the right quarter as charted. Place areas in the left quarter in the same relation to the horizontal centre, but in reverse relation to the vertical centre.

3. To work the lower quarters, hold the chart upside-down (as it is shown in the illustration below) as you use it to locate the areas at the bottom.

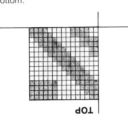

TOP

4. Place areas in the left quarter as charted. Place areas in the right quarter in the same relation to the horizontal centre, but in reverse to the vertical centre.

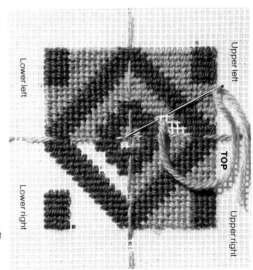

TOP · Lower left · Upper left · Lower right · Upper right

TO ALTERNATE STITCH DIRECTION WITH EACH QUARTER

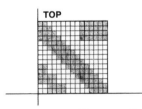

TOP

1. Work the upper right quarter with top edge of chart at top. Locate areas on chart; work them in same positions on canvas.

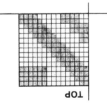

TOP

2. To work lower left quarter, turn chart upside-down. Find areas on chart; work them as they are positioned on upside-down chart.

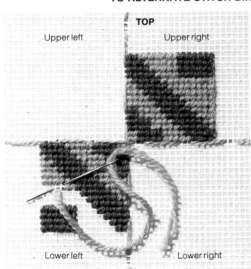

TOP · Upper left · Upper right · Lower left · Lower right

3. To work the upper left quarter, hold the canvas with its top edge at the side. Read the worked upper right quarter to locate areas, and place them in the upper left quarter in the same relation to the horizontal centre of the canvas but in the reverse relation to its vertical centre.

4. To work the lower right quarter, hold the canvas with its top edge at the side. Read the worked lower left quarter to locate the areas, and place them in the lower right quarter in the same relation to the horizontal centre of the canvas but in the reverse relation to its vertical centre.

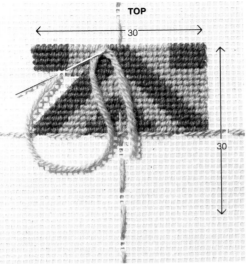

63

Designing and making canvas work

Repeat patterns

A motif repeated a number of times according to a planned arrangement is a repeat pattern. The motif can be anything you like that makes an attractive pattern when it is repeated systematically. Before a design is worked, the arrangement must be planned and the basic motif charted. The chart must have a thread count that, when multiplied, permits the arrangement to fit a finished canvas size. To calculate motif size for charting, see opposite page.

The motif can be your own design or a tracing from an existing source, perhaps a ready-made chart. If the source is a chart, it may turn out that its thread count will fit or can be altered to fit the arrangement. If it is a half-chart or quarter-chart, follow the procedures on the right to obtain a complete shape. Make several copies of the motif, either by re-tracing it or using a photocopying machine. Trim away excess paper, leaving a border if you want a background. Position the copies different ways until you find a satisfactory arrangement.

Although many repeat arrangements are possible, the three at the bottom of the page are the most common. In the first, a **straight** arrangement, the units in the rows line up horizontally and vertically. In the second and third arrangements, the units are staggered. To achieve a **horizontally staggered** arrangement, line up the vertical centres of the units in every horizontal row with the ends of the units in the row above. For a **half-drop** arrangement, line up the horizontal centres of the units in every vertical row with the ends of the units in the row to the left. Be prepared to encounter partial motifs, which can occur with any arrangement, particularly those that are staggered.

When you have an arrangement you like, place tracing paper over it and trace all lines. Use this tracing when calculating the size of the motif and working the arrangement on canvas.

Producing a single motif

A complete motif can be your own original drawing, or a motif traced from a book, a piece of fabric, or even a ready-made full design chart.

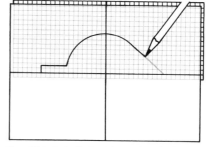

If motif is in half-chart form, draw horizontal and vertical lines on tracing paper and align them with centre lines on chart. Trace charted half.

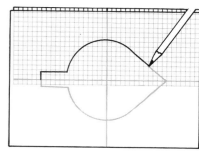

To form second half, turn tracing paper, positioning unmarked half over chart. Match lines on tracing paper and chart; re-trace chart.

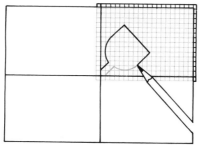

If motif is in quarter-chart form, draw horizontal and vertical lines on tracing paper and match them with lines on chart. Trace charted quarter.

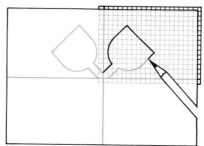

To trace second quarter, turn tracing paper so that unmarked quarter is over chart. Match lines on tracing paper and chart; re-trace quarter.

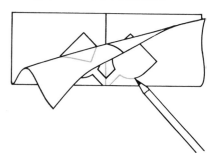

To form second half, fold tracing paper in half so that unmarked half is over drawn half of design. Re-trace design half; open tracing paper.

Types of arrangements

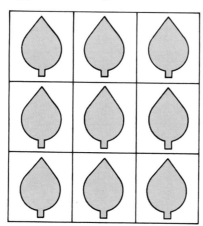

Straight arrangement

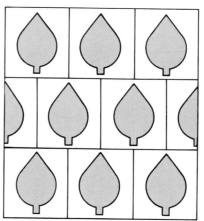

Horizontally staggered arrangement

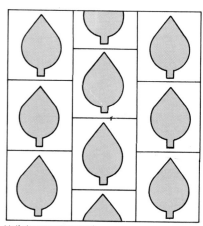

Half-drop arrangement

Calculating unit size; working repeat patterns

To chart an original motif for a repeat-pattern design, you must first decide its area in the arrangement, then its thread size. The area is the length and width of one unit; thread size is the number of canvas threads spanned by this area. To calculate the length of a unit, divide the finished length of the canvas by the number of unit rows up and down. To determine the width, divide the finished width of the canvas by the number of rows across. To find the thread size of the unit, multiply its length and width by the gauge of the canvas. Canvas gauge should be suitable to the needs of the design and to the durability requirements of the finished item (pp. 6, 56–57). Once thread size is known, the motif can be charted (next page). Example A is a lesson in simple calculation. If you have traced an existing chart to obtain your motif, its thread size may fit exactly into the finished size of the arrangement. If it does not, perhaps the thread count of the finished size or of the chart can be altered. If the charted motif has no background, try changing the

arrangement's finished size or select a different gauge of canvas (Example B) to provide the number of threads needed for the chart's repetition. For a chart that has a background area, try increasing or decreasing the number of background threads to arrive at a new thread size that will fit the finished thread count (Example C, background area was increased). Sometimes, no matter what you do, the ready-made chart will not fit. If you find yourself in this situation, choose another motif.

To prepare to work a repeat-pattern design, cut canvas to contain the total number of threads needed for the arrangement plus a minimum 5 cm margin at each edge. Tape all edges; label the top edge. Also mark the horizontal and vertical lines of the arrangement; units are worked within their boundaries. Use the chart to work at least the first unit; to work the others, follow either the chart or a worked unit. For partial units work just the portion required by the arrangement (see Example B, on right).

EXAMPLE B

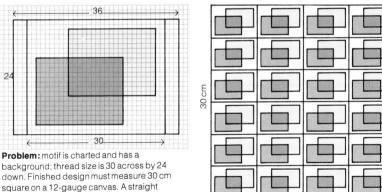

Problem: finished design must measure 30 cm wide by 35 cm long on either a 12 or 14-gauge canvas. Motif is from a ready-made chart that has a thread size of 28 across by 28 down. A horizontally staggered arrangement is planned, with 6 units across by 7 down.

Solution: since each of the units as charted requires 28 threads by 28 threads, the planned arrangement of 6 units across by 7 down will need a total of 168 threads across by 196 up and down. A piece of 12-gauge canvas measuring 30 cm wide by 35 cm long (size of finished design) contains 144 threads across by 168 up and down; this is not enough threads for the units as charted and planned. A piece of 14-gauge canvas 30 cm wide by 35 cm long contains 168 threads across by 196 up and down; this is the exact number of threads needed for the units as charted and planned. It makes sense, therefore, to use the motif as charted and work the arrangement as planned on a 14-gauge canvas. When working the partial units in the staggered rows, be sure to work the chart's right half at the left end of the row and the chart's left half at the right end of the row.

EXAMPLE A

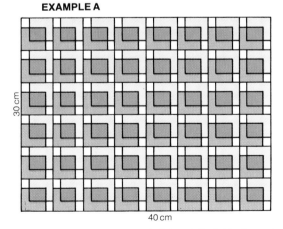

Problem: finished item must measure 40 cm wide by 30 cm long on a 10 or 12-gauge canvas. Motif is original and in a straight arrangement of 8 units across by 6 down.

Solution: in order for a planned straight arrangement of 8 units across by 6 down to fit a finished area of 40 cm wide and 30 cm long, each unit must measure 5 cm by 5 cm. If a 10-gauge canvas is used for the entire design, each unit will span 20 by 20 threads; if canvas is 12-gauge, each unit will span 24 by 24 threads. Chart motif according to the gauge of canvas that the entire arrangement will be worked on. For instructions on charting, see next page.

EXAMPLE C

Problem: motif is charted and has a background; thread size is 30 across by 24 down. Finished design must measure 30 cm square on a 12-gauge canvas. A straight arrangement, 4 units by 6 down, is planned.

Solution: a 30 cm square of 12-gauge canvas contains 144 by 144 threads. If the chart (thread size of 30 across by 24 down) is used to work the arrangement as planned (4 units across by 6 down), it will span 120 threads across by 144 down (24 threads short of the finished width; correct number for length). If 6 threads of background are added to the width of each of the 4 units (3 on each end of each unit), the 144 threads will be spanned. Add 3 threads to each side of chart.

Designing and making canvas work

Charting a design

Before charting your own design, you should familiarise yourself with the types of designs and how they are presented in chart form. You should also understand the two ways canvas threads are represented in charts and how symbols and keys are used to indicate the stitch and colour. All of this information is on pp. 60–65.

To chart your own design, first decide on its finished size and then determine the number of canvas threads that will be required to carry out the full design or the repeated part. This procedure has been explained for a repeat pattern (p. 65). Single-motif designs usually must be enlarged or reduced to fit the finished size (this is most easily achieved with a photocopier). Draw one line across and another line down the centre of the re-sized drawing; label its top edge. Decide what gauge of canvas is suitable for the needs of the design (pp. 56–57) and cut a piece to the finished size plus a minimum 5 cm margin on each edge. Bind its edges with tape; label the top edge; mark vertical and horizontal centres (p. 61).

Centre the prepared drawing under the prepared canvas, then count the canvas threads spanned by the entire design or the repeated part. If the design is *asymmetrical*, count the number of threads across and up and down the entire design. For a *horizontal two-way symmetrical* design, count only the top half from side to side and from the centre up. For a *vertical two-way symmetrical* design, count the right half from top to bottom and from the centre out. For a *four-way symmetrical* design, count threads only for the top right quarter of the design, from its horizontal centre to the top and from its vertical centre out to the right edge.

When the thread size of the design is established, you duplicate it within the same number of squares or lines on graph paper. When charting the motif for a repeat pattern, place a finished-size drawing of it under its prepared canvas and proceed with Step 2, below.

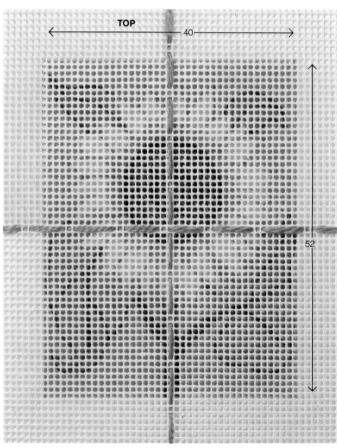

1. Centre finished-size drawing of design under prepared canvas. Pin layers in place; count canvas threads spanned by design or design part across and down.

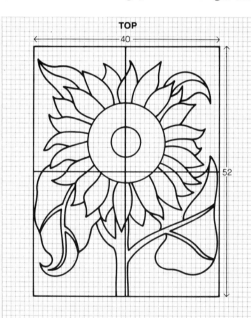

2. On graph paper (any gauge), count the threads called for by design or part being charted. On a box chart, a square is a 'thread'; on a line chart, a line is a 'thread'. Draw box around this number of threads; draw centre lines for design or part being charted: both lines for full design, as above; for horizontal half, a vertical centre line from bottom of box; for vertical half, a horizontal centre line from left side of box.

3. Referring to the design under the canvas, draw the lines of the design over the lines on the graph paper, making sure they cross the graph paper lines just as they do the canvas threads. Use a pencil and draw an area at a time, using the centre lines on canvas and graph paper as reference points.

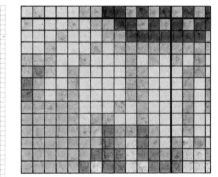

Make a box chart if you intend to use only tent stitches. Re-draw the lines in steps along the nearest squares. Fill squares with intended colours or use symbols and make a colour key.

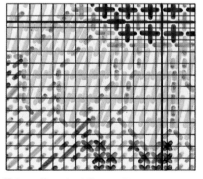

Make a line chart if you will use ornamental stitches. Sketch intended stitch in design area, then modify the area's lines to fit the stitches (p. 59). Draw stitches in actual colours or use symbols to denote colour and make a colour key.

Designing and working Florentine embroidery

Types of Florentine work
Florentine stitch patterns
Colour
Equipment
Row designs
Motif designs
Four-way designs

Types of Florentine work

Florentine work is defined, in the most general terms, as any design worked on canvas with straight stitches. By this broad definition, any design, even the sunflower opposite, becomes Florentine work if straight stitches are used to work it on to the canvas. Traditionally, however, the name Florentine work signifies a unique form of canvas work in which Florentine stitch or one of its variations is used to produce dramatic patterns on canvas. It is this traditional kind of Florentine embroidery that is described on the following pages.

There are three fundamental types of Florentine-based designs, represented by the three examples on the right. Each of the three overall designs is formed through the repeated working of a single unit (for clarity, the repeated unit is outlined in each example). To ensure that the unit is the same each time it is worked, the unit is charted; such a chart is called a *row chart*. The three designs differ mainly in the character of their repeat units. In a **row design** (first example), the repeat unit consists of several rows of Florentine stitches that follow the pattern established by the top row. For a more detailed explanation of designing and working a row design, see pp. 70–71. In a **motif design** (second example), the top and bottom rows of the repeat unit mirror each other and together form an enclosed intervening area. This area is filled with Florentine stitches or other straight stitches that conform to the area's shape. Motif designs are explained on pp. 72–73. The third type is a **four-way design,** in which the overall design is produced by working each triangular quarter of the design at right-angles to the others. Although a row design repeat is the basic unit in the four-way design shown, a motif design unit can also be used to form this type of Florentine work. The design and working of four-way Florentine designs are dealt with on pp. 74–76.

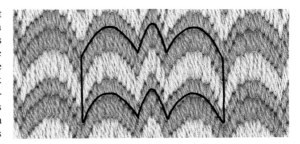

Row designs are the easiest of the Florentine types to design and work. The repeat unit consists of several rows of Florentine stitches that follow the pattern of the top row of the repeat. The overall effect is bands of mirror-imaging repeats across the canvas.

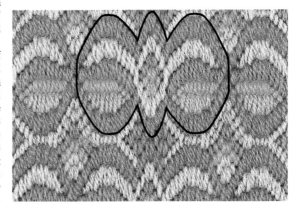

Motif designs form medallion-like repeats across the canvas. The repeat consists of a top and bottom row that mirror each other and form an enclosed area. This area is filled with Florentine or other straight stitches.

Four-way designs are produced by working the triangular quarters of the overall design at right-angles to each other. Either a row or motif type of repeat can be used to form the design. The design shown here is based on a row type of repeat.

Designing and working Florentine embroidery

Forming Florentine stitch patterns

Even though there are only three fundamental types of Florentine-based designs, the number of possible patterns among them is almost limitless. This is because the span of Florentine stitches on which a repeat unit is based can be varied in many ways. Some knowledge of how these variations are achieved will help you to design your own project, or more easily to understand and work a design from a ready-made row chart.

The zigzag pattern of any Florentine stitch is formed by combining two elements: straight Gobelin stitches and a stitch-placing device known as *step*. Step allows the stitches to be placed diagonally next to each other so that the stitches can rise to form the peaks or descend to form the valleys of the zigzag pattern. The illustrations below show the effects of stitch length and step on the height of a peak. Under each example is a set of

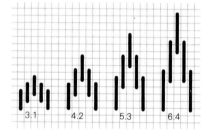

Effects of stitch length and step on peak height.

numbers. The first number denotes stitch length; the second, the amount of step between stitches. Stitches can be from two to eight threads long. Step, which is the number of threads between the bases of neighbouring stitches, must be at least one less than the stitch length number. As the examples show, the greater the stitch length and step, the higher the peak (or lower the valley). The extremes would be even greater if more than three stitches were used between peak and valley.

The row pattern of a Florentine stitch

is formed by combining peaks and valleys. If peaks and valleys are all the same size, the result is an even zigzag pattern, which is the Florentine stitch at its most basic. When pointed peaks and valleys of different sizes are combined, a variation of the Florentine stitch, known as flame stitch, is produced. Additional

The basic Florentine stitch produces an even zigzag pattern. This is achieved by combining peaks and valleys of the same size. To form a deep zigzag pattern, use high, same-size peaks and valleys; for a shallow zigzag, use short, same-size peaks and valleys.

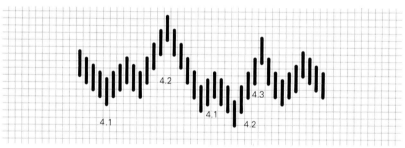

To form an uneven zigzag pattern, combine peaks and valleys of different sizes. Stitches in example above are all four threads long, but heights of peaks and valleys are varied by using different numbers of stitches between them, and changing the amount of step between the stitches.

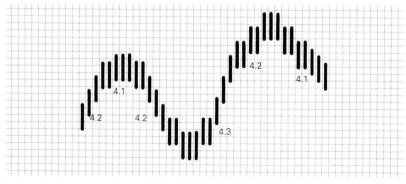

Peaks and valleys can be rounded by using blocks of straight Gobelin stitches at their tips or between them. Step is retained between blocks but not between the individual stitches of a block.

variation can be achieved in a zigzag pattern by rounding the points. This is done by using blocks of straight Gobelin stitches. There can be from two to six stitches in a block; the blocks can be placed at the tip of a peak or valley or between the two. The step is kept between blocks but not between stitches.

Colour

The most basic role of colour in Florentine work is identifying rows or areas in the repeat unit, a natural result of each row or area usually being assigned its own colour. Properly selected and placed in the repeat unit, however, colour can also add depth or movement to the overall design. Colours cause different visual responses; you can control these by assigning colour to a row or area according to how much you want it to stand out in the design. To select colours so that they will perform to your satisfaction, it helps to know something about colour theory.

There are six basic colours in a colour wheel – red, yellow, orange, blue, green and violet. The first three (red, yellow and orange) tend to stand out in a design; the last three (blue, green and violet) tend to recede. Each of these colours has a range of tones, that is, degrees of lightness and darkness. A light tone, or *tint*, is achieved by adding white to the colour. To produce a dark tone, or *shade*, black is added to the colour. As a general rule, tints appear to come forward and shades to go back. How much a tint comes forward or a shade goes back will depend on the intensity of the pure colour from which it was derived. For example, pink, which is a tint of red, will advance more than will pale blue, which is a tint of blue.

The power of any colour or tone is affected by colours and tones around it. A harmonious combination is one in which colours are close, producing a relaxed visual response. A contrasting combination, in which the colours are not close, produces an active response. Most harmonious of all is a combination involving variations of a single colour. Also harmonious is a scheme of related colours, such as blue with blue-green and green. Contrasting schemes may consist of contrasts in tone (very light against very dark) or in colour (violet, green and orange).

SHADES AND TINTS

Shades (darker tones), formed by adding black.

Pure red   Pure blue

Tints (lighter tones), formed by adding white.

KINDS OF COLOUR SCHEMES

Harmonious colour schemes. To form a monochrome harmony, combine several close values of one colour as was done in the first sample above. To create an analogous harmony, combine several related colours as in the second example above.

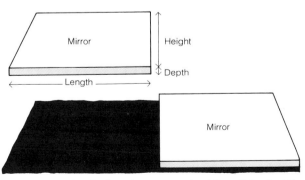

Contrasting colour schemes may be produced by combining distant tones of one colour as shown by the example on the left. Or, to get a complementary contrasting scheme, combine unrelated colours as was done in the example on the right.

RELATED/UNRELATED COLOURS

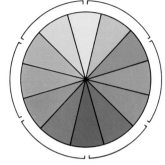

Related colours are those that are next to each other on the colour wheel – red, red-orange and orange; blue, blue-violet and violet.

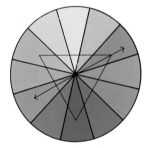

Unrelated colours are those that are opposite or separated on the wheel. Red and green are unrelated; so are green, orange and violet.

Equipment

To work a Florentine embroidery, you will require a chart of the design, canvas and thread. Since this embroidery is a type of repeat pattern design, the amount of canvas needed will be a multiple of the number of threads in the chart. The procedures for estimating canvas amounts are explained on the next few pages. If you are designing your own Florentine embroidery, you will need graph paper and colouring pens. A very handy designing tool is a set of projection mirrors. You can make a set yourself (see right) with felt, glue and two identical small mirrors.

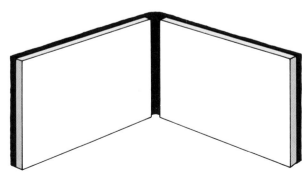

To make a set of projection mirrors, proceed as follows. Cut a piece of felt that is as wide as the mirror is high and equal in length to twice the mirror's combined length and depth (thickness).

Spread glue on wrong side of both mirrors. Position a mirror at each end of the felt, glued side down. Press both of the mirrors in place and wipe off any excess glue. Leave to dry before using.

Designing and working Florentine embroidery

Row design charts

The first step in designing any of the three types of Florentine embroidery designs is to establish the row pattern on which the repeat unit will be based. The easiest way to find a row pattern is to slide projection mirrors (see p. 69) along a predetermined row of Florentine stitches. Though any row of Florentine stitches can serve this purpose (even a photograph of a finished sample), you can improve your chances of discovering a unique pattern by experimenting with a stitch row that you designed (p. 68). The way the mirrors should be held to reflect the kind of establishing row pattern you need will depend on the type of unit you are designing. The plotting of row design units is explained here; for motif and four-way design units, refer to pp. 72, 74 and 75.

To plan a row design unit, you need to establish a side-to-side pattern for the top row. You can find one by sliding a mirror along a charted row of stitches (Steps 2 and 3 below). Slide it from right to left and from left to right; patterns will differ each way. More patterns can be produced by turning the row upside-down. When you have found a satisfactory top row, make a line chart of it (p. 60 on a new piece of graph paper; then chart the other rows of the repeat under the first (Steps 4, 5 and 6). Each new row can have a different stitch length so long as the length used will maintain the step arrangement established by the top row. When charting, use a different colour for each row. Colours need not match those in which the design will be worked on the canvas; once the actual colour arrangement is decided, however, it should be indicated on the chart.

When designing your own unit, it is recommended that you chart the entire side-to-side pattern of all the rows of the unit, this lets you see the actual pattern. Many ready-made charts depict only half of the side-to-side pattern.

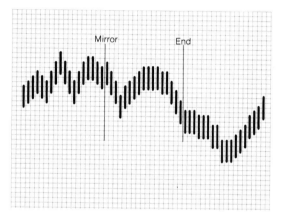

1. Begin by charting a row of Florentine stitches. Make the row long enough to include peaks and valleys of several different sizes and shapes. The red lines indicate position of mirror and end of side-to-side pattern established in Step 3.

2. Position one mirror parallel to the charted stitches. Slowly slide the mirror along the row, looking, as you do, at the charted stitches and their mirrored images. Stop when you come to a section that forms a pleasing pattern on each side of the mirror.

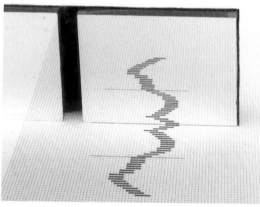

3. Holding the mirror in place and still looking at the charted stitches and their images, slide your finger along charted stitches until you come to a suitable end to the side-to-side pattern. Mark the end with a line; make another line along edge of mirror.

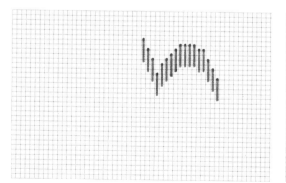

4. On a new piece of graph paper, chart the stitches that lie between the marks drawn in Step 3. When making the new chart, be sure to draw the stitches to the same length and step, and in the same positions, as they were on the original chart.

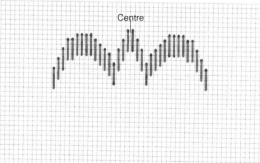

5. Then chart the mirror images of the stitches. These are charted in the opposite direction from those in Step 4 but in the same order. Make sure that you also chart them to the same stitch length and step. Mark the centre of the side-to-side charted pattern.

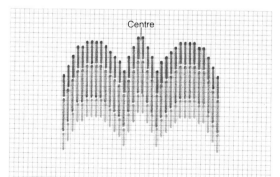

6. Using a different colour for each, chart the other rows of the unit under the first. For each row, use a stitch length that will maintain the step arrangement established by the top row (note that 3-stitch length is too short for the 3-step in centre peak).

Preparing for and working a row design

Florentine designs look best with units centred on the canvas. You can centre a row design by centring the top row at the vertical centre of the canvas (drawing A), or by placing a top row on each side (drawing B). Because of unevenness in heights, most row patterns will cross the horizontal centre irregularly.

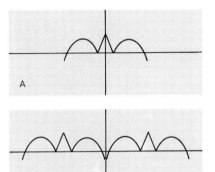

With the centre position determined, decide on the number of units you want across and up and down for the total design; then calculate the canvas threads needed to work the design. To find the number of threads needed across, multiply the number of units across by the number of threads across one unit. To find the number needed for length, multiply the number of row units up and down the design by the number of threads needed for each row. Divide these totals by your canvas gauge; the resulting numbers are the measurements of the finished canvas. If the arrangement and gauge produce too small a finished size, add full or partial units to enlarge it. If they produce too large a size, reduce the number of units or select a finer canvas gauge. Prepare canvas for work by cutting it to finished size plus a minimum 5 cm margin along each edge; tape all edges and label the top; mark centres (p. 61).

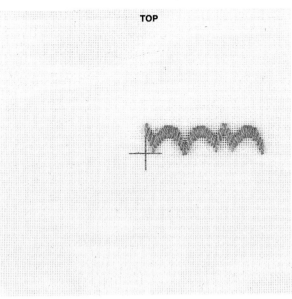

1. Start at centre of canvas; work the top row of each unit planned for right half of design. Refer to chart for colour and stitch placing.

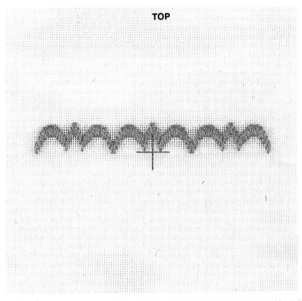

2. Begin again at centre and work the top row of each unit planned for left half of design. Check entire span for accuracy of stitch placing.

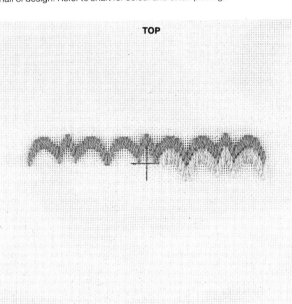

3. Using the row just completed as a guide, work the second row of all units in one journey across the canvas. Refer to chart for row colour.

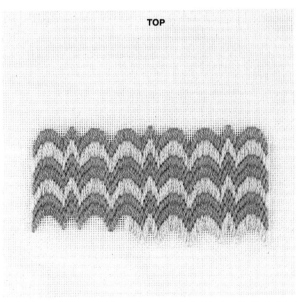

4. Work remaining rows of lower, then upper half of design. Begin each row at right or left edge; refer to chart for its correct colour.

Designing and working Florentine embroidery

Motif design charts

To design a repeat unit of the motif type, you need to establish patterns for both top and bottom rows. The rows are identical, and are found simultaneously by holding projection mirrors (p. 69) at right-angles to each other and to a row of Florentine stitches. As shown in Step 2 below, a side-to-side pattern is formed on each side of the vertical mirror and this same row pattern is also seen upside-down in both mirrors. When top and bottom rows are in this relationship, an open area is formed between them. This area is filled with Florentine or other straight stitches. With many of the motif patterns, open areas between rows will themselves form secondary motifs. When designing your own motif, it is recommended that you chart several motifs, as shown in Step 4, so that you can see and plan the design of the secondary motifs. Many ready-made charts show only half of both primary and secondary motifs.

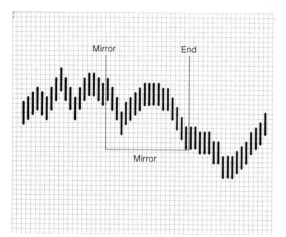

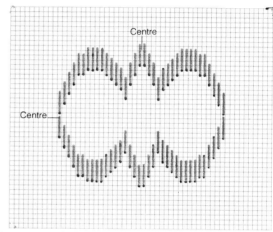

1. Chart a row of Florentine stitches long enough to include various sizes and shapes of peaks and valleys (p. 68). Red lines indicate the positions of the mirrors and the end of the side-to-side pattern established in the next step.

2. With mirrors at right-angles to each other and stitches, slide them along row until you find a suitable motif pattern. To adjust motif depth, slide mirrors up and down. Mark end of side-to-side pattern; trace right-angle formed by edges of both mirrors.

3. Re-chart stitches between marks; draw stitches intersected by horizontal line to the length above the intersection. Chart other half of side-to-side pattern and mark centre (p. 70). Chart bottom row to mirror top row; mark horizontal centre of motif.

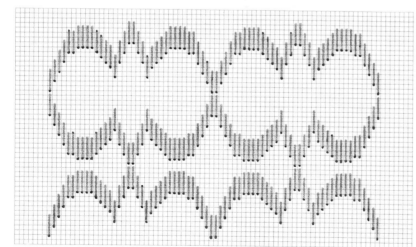

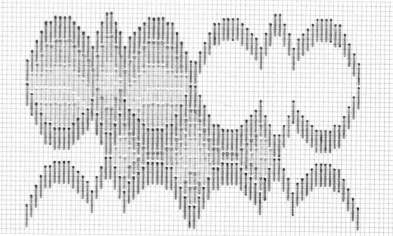

4. To determine if open areas between rows of motifs will form secondary motifs, chart another motif next to the first; under these, chart the top row of two corresponding motifs, aligning their vertical centres with centres of motifs above, and abutting highest points below with lowest points above.

5. Fill in on your chart the open areas of the primary and secondary motifs with Florentine stitches or other straight stitches that make interesting patterns and conform to the shapes of the open areas. Use a different colour for each row or area.

Preparing and working a motif design

The centring of motif design units is usually achieved either by centring a motif at the exact centre of the canvas (drawing A), or by placing full motifs at each side of the centres (drawing B).

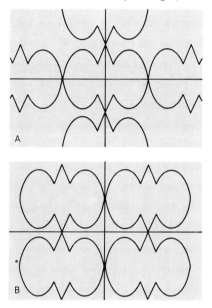

Some motif designs, however, combine these two arrangements. For example, the design on the right centres the motifs horizontally, but places full motifs on each side of the vertical centre. When the centring is determined, decide how many units you want across and up and down to form the total design. Then calculate the amount of canvas needed, and prepare it for working.

As shown in Step 1 on the right, the first row to be worked is the top row of the motifs that run across the centre. If you want the centres of the motifs to be at the horizontal centre of the canvas, then work this top row along the horizontal centre. If you prefer to have whole motifs above the horizontal centre, you will need to work the top row a full motif above that centre line.

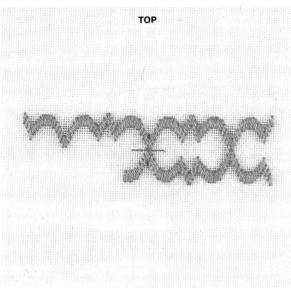

TOP

1. Work top row of motifs from vertical centre out to each edge; work bottom row in one journey across. Placing depends on unit centring plan.

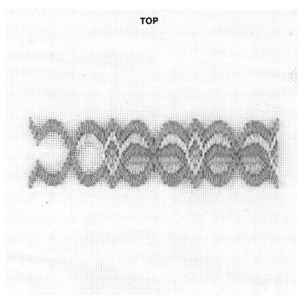

TOP

2. Referring to chart for colour and stitch position, work middle areas of motifs – either one at a time or parts of all progressively.

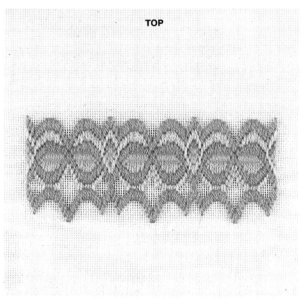

TOP

3. Work top row of next span of motifs in one journey across canvas. Work the middle areas of secondary motifs one at a time or progressively.

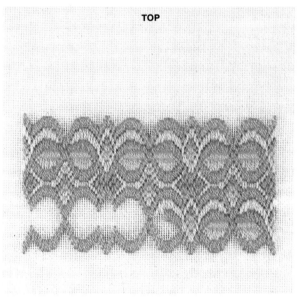

TOP

4. Continue to work this way – that is, work a row, then the middle areas – until lower half of the design, then upper half, are completed.

Designing and working Florentine embroidery

Four-way row design charts

Four-way Florentine work consists of four identical triangular quarters that meet and change direction along diagonal lines. Because of this structure, it is also known as mitred Florentine. To design your own four-way Florentine, you need only chart one whole quarter; you then follow it four times to work the design. The design of the quarter can be based on a row design unit, as on this page, or a motif design (opposite page). The main difference between the charting of the two types is the way the row or motif is established and centred in the triangular quarter. To work either type of four-way design, see p. 76.

1. Design a row of Florentine stitches (row above is the same as on p. 70). Hold one mirror parallel to stitches; other at a 45° angle to first. Move mirrors along stitches to find a four-way side-to-side row pattern; up and down to alter length of pattern and its distance from centre of design. Trace 45° angle along mirrors to mark first half of row pattern and its distance from centre.

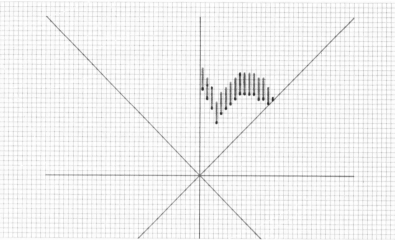

2. On a new piece of graph paper, draw vertical and horizontal centre lines; mitre quarters as shown. If row pattern has one stitch at centre, draw lines *between* graph lines; if row has same number of stitches on each side of centre, draw lines *on* graph lines. Chart first half of row same distance above centre as marked in stage 1; draw stitches intersected by diagonal mark to length above intersection.

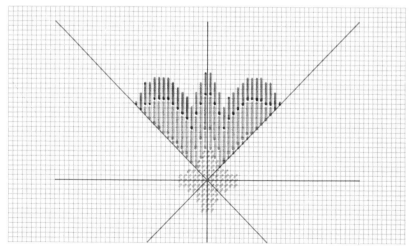

3. Chart second half of row to mirror first half (p. 70). Maintaining pattern set by the first row, chart progressively shorter rows towards centre of design. If space between diagonals becomes too short to chart an acceptable row pattern, design an arrangement of tent or ornamental stitches to fill rest of centre area. Chart all quarters of centre design; for another treatment, see next page.

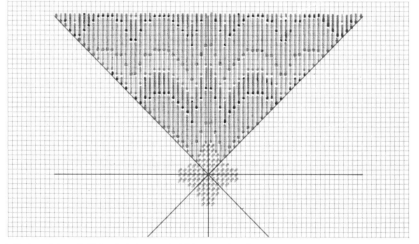

4. Design wide end of triangle to form a straight outer edge. Ornamental or tent stitches can be used (see next page), or you can chart increasingly longer side-to-side row patterns as shown here. If charting rows, maintain pattern set by first; make rows longer by charting stitches to mirror the ends of the row patterns. Use filling-in stitches and parts of rows to form straight edge.

Four-way motif design charts

The primary consideration, in charting a four-way design, is that the establishing row or motif be centred in a triangle. A row design is automatically centred in the process of designing four-way row patterns (Step 1, facing page). When a motif is used for a four-way design, design the top and bottom rows of the motif first (Step 1 below) and then establish its centre position in the triangle (Step 2). This must be done in two stages because there is no way to hold projection mirrors so that they simultaneously reflect both the top and bottom rows of a motif and the motif's arrangement in a four-way pattern.

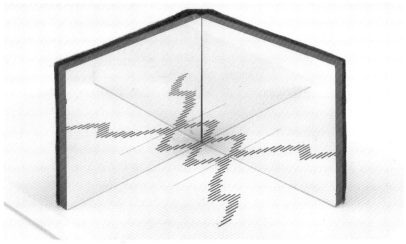

1. Design a row of Florentine stitches (the row used above is different from the one on pp. 70 and 72). With mirrors at right-angles to each other and to the stitches, slide them along the stitches until you find a suitable motif. Slide mirrors up and down if you wish to alter motif depth. Mark the end of the side-to-side pattern; trace the right-angle formed by the mirrors.

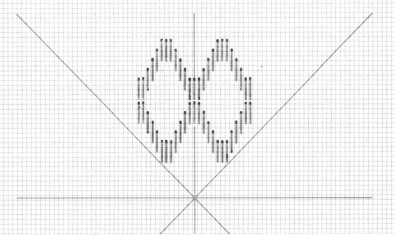

2. Chart top and bottom rows of motif (see p. 72); draw a line down vertical centre of motif. Directly under motif, draw diagonal mitre lines. Mitre lines should meet at the vertical centre line and form a 45° angle on each side of that line; they should not intersect any stitches of the motif. Draw a horizontal centre line through point where diagonals meet vertical centre line.

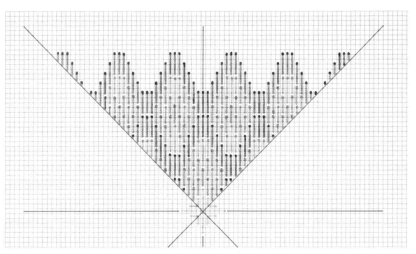

3. If upper portion of motif does not fully span the distance between diagonals, chart partial motifs to fill spaces. Chart middle of each motif, then chart rows and a centre treatment to fill the space (if any) between motif and centre of design. Chart all four quarters of the centre treatment (ornamental stitches are used here; design on facing page has tent stitches at its centre).

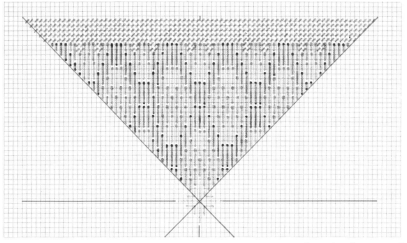

4. Design the wide end of the triangle, making its outer edge straight. Depending on the effect you want, either chart full, then partial rows above motif (as was done above establishing row in Step 4, opposite page), or plan to fill the space above the motif with tent or ornamental stitches, or use a combination of partial rows and other stitches, as was done here.

Designing and working Florentine embroidery

Preparing for and working a four-way design

The centring of the units in a four-way Florentine design is established in its chart and should be maintained in all four quarters of the design as you work them. To work the full design, you have to determine the amount of canvas needed to contain it. To do this, first calculate the number of threads at the outer edge of the triangle, then divide this number by the gauge of your canvas. This one measurement is all that is needed because the outer edges of the triangles are the same on all four sides of the finished design. Some ready-made charts show adjacent halves of triangles separated by a diagonal or mitre line (see the illustration of such a chart below). If you are using this type of chart, calculate the total number of threads for the outer

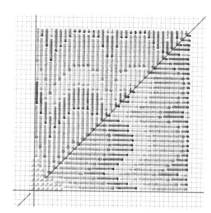

edge of a whole triangle by doubling the number of threads charted for the outer edge of one of the halves.

Cut a piece of canvas to measure the finished length and width plus a minimum 5 cm margin along each edge. Tape all edges and label the top edge. Mark the centres of the canvas (see p. 61). Use wool tackings to mark the lines of the design. Although a row design is being worked on the right, the same procedures apply for a four-way motif design.

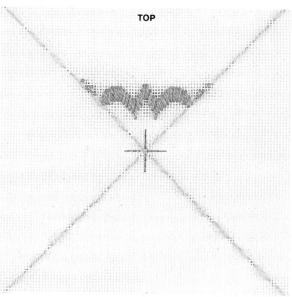

1. Begin with top quarter and work its middle row from vertical centre out to each mitre line. Refer to chart for colour and stitch position.

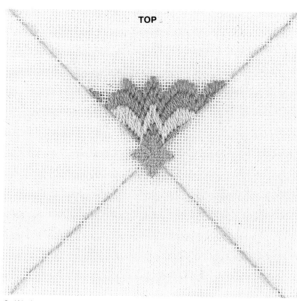

2. Work remaining rows from mitre to mitre; first those from middle row down; then entire centre treatment; finally top rows to outer edge.

3. Turn canvas clockwise and work rows of next quarter in any convenient sequence. Be sure rows match their counterparts along the mitre.

4. Work third and fourth quarters as the second quarter was done. Refer to chart or a worked quarter for colour and stitch position.

General working techniques

Calculating thread amounts

The amount of thread needed to work a particular design will depend on the stitches and the gauge of the canvas as well as the planned finished size of the design. In order to calculate the total thread requirements, you have to determine the amount of thread each stitch uses to cover a square centimetre of canvas. If you plan to use only one stitch, only one test is necessary; if several stitches are being used, you must test them all. All stitch tests must be done on the same gauge of canvas as the

design will be worked on. You must also use the proper weight of thread for the stitch and the canvas gauge (see p. 12).

To do a stitch test, cut your thread into several 50 cm (half metre) lengths. Using the pre-measured lengths, work a 2 cm square of the stitch. Record how many lengths were used and convert this number into metres; if a partial length was used, count it as a full length. Use the test result amount to calculate the total amount of thread needed for that particular stitch over the entire design.

Estimate how many square centimetres of that stitch will be worked in the design and multiply that number by the test result amount. Apportion this total amount among the different colours in which the test stitch will be worked. Apply the test result amount of each stitch test in the same way. Add the amounts for individual colours to arrive at the total amount needed for each. To allow for mistakes in calculation or during the work, increase each colour's amount by 10 per cent.

Removing stitches

Stitching mistakes are likely to happen, and are no cause for alarm. If you notice the error while you are stitching and it involves only two or three stitches, the correction is easy. Unthread the needle, pull out the incorrect stitches and re-stitch them with the same thread. If the mistake involves more than just a few simple stitches, or if you discover it after the area is finished, the procedure is different. In this case, you have to carefully cut the incorrect stitches from the canvas, as shown and explained on the right, then, with new thread, re-stitch the area where stitches were cut.

1. From right side, slip scissors blade under a few incorrect stitches; pull thread up from canvas and cut. Clip a few at a time until all are cut.

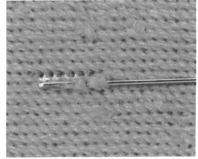

2. From wrong side, with eye end of needle, pull out cut thread. To secure intact stitches, unstitch a few; catch thread into backs of new stitches.

Repairing ripped canvas

You may discover that in the process of removing stitches you have accidentally cut the threads of the canvas. If this happens, you can easily repair the cut with a patch of the same canvas type and gauge. To prepare the area for the repair, pull out enough stitches around the cut to allow ample space for the patch. A patch needs to be a few meshes larger each way than the cut; the space for the patch must be slightly larger than the patch. When the area is ready, apply the patch as shown and explained on the right. Re-stitch the area through both layers; trim threads that protrude.

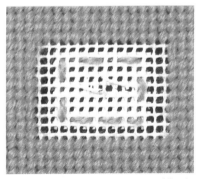

1. Position canvas patch under the cut. Align the threads of both canvases; tack patch in place.

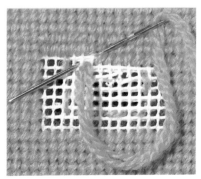

2. Re-stitch area through both layers of canvas. Carefully trim any protruding canvas threads.

General working techniques

Setting canvas into a frame

It is best to do canvas work on a frame or other holding device. Work that is done this way will stay neat and be less distorted when it is finished. As explained on p. 10, there are different types of frames and stretchers, each with its own use and limitations. Basic instructions for setting canvas into most of the frames are given below. A fine-gauge canvas can be set into a hoop if you prefer; for instructions, see the Embroidery chapter. Because there will be slight variations among different brands of frames, you should use these instructions as guides, adapting them if necessary to your needs. If your frame is equipped with a stand, you should attach it before starting to work.

Slate and rotating types are the most versatile of all the canvas work frames. Each consists of top and bottom rods and two side arms (see the illustrations below). The canvas is attached to fabric tapes on the rods, and the rods are then inserted into the side arms. If your slate or rotating frame does not have fabric tapes, you should add them.

To add fabric tapes, cut two lengths of rug binding or webbing, each slightly longer than rod after insertion into side arms. Centre tape on rod with one edge lapped and the other extending; turn raw edges of tape under flush with working ends of rod. Secure lapped edge with staples or small tacks. Attach the second tape the same way.

SLATE FRAME

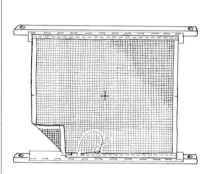 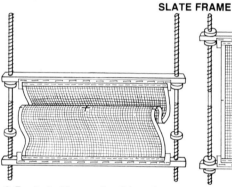 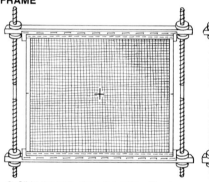 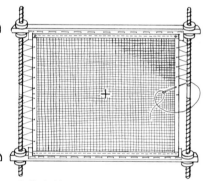

1. Centre and lap the top canvas edge over the tape on the top rod; hold in place. Sew the canvas firmly to the tape with a needle and strong thread (such as button thread) using backstitches. Use several backstitches in one place to start to secure the thread, and several more at the end to prevent the canvas becoming undone when under tension.

2. To attach side arms, the distance between rods must be less than the side arms' length but no less than half that length. If necessary, roll canvas on to one or both rods. Place a locking nut on each end of each side arm; bring to centres. Insert top ends of arms into ends of top rod; slip arms through and insert other ends into bottom rod.

3. Slide the rods along the arms with canvas centred in the frame. Bring the centred nuts out to hold the rods in place, holding the canvas taut. Attach a nut to each end of each arm; bring towards the rods. Tighten all the locking nuts. Some slate frames have slat side arms with spaced holes. The canvas is held taut by pegs through rods in the appropriate holes.

4. To hold canvas taut at the sides, oversew each side to an arm. Begin and end by winding thread between nut and rod. When finished, adjust thread to hold canvas evenly. If preferred, use tape and pins. To reposition canvas, remove oversewing and repeat Steps 2 to 4. Keep canvas evenly tensioned to prevent unnecessary distortion.

ROTATING FRAME

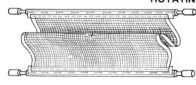

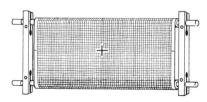

1. Secure top and bottom edges of canvas to webbing on top and bottom rods as explained in Step 1 of slate frame instructions (see above). Loosen wing nuts at ends of side arms and slip the rods through openings in the arms.

2. Turn rods to take up slack canvas; secure by tightening nuts. Edges can be oversewn to side arms (Step 4 above). To re-position canvas, remove oversewing and loosen nuts; re-roll canvas and tighten nuts.

CANVAS STRETCHER

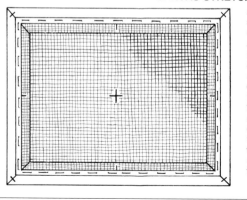

Arrange the four strips as they will be set together, each with its shorter edge towards the inside of the frame. At each of the four corners, fit ends of adjacent strips together and staple across each join to secure it. Mark centre of each strip. Centre canvas over frame, making sure that the entire working area is clear of the frame's inner edges. Allow a margin of 2 cm all round. Staple or pin each edge of the canvas to the frame. Canvas should not be re-positioned after work has begun. This would mean stapling or pinning through some of the worked area.

Blocking canvas work

Blocking is the process that brings the stitched canvas work to its original size and alignment. It is made necessary by the almost unavoidable distortion that occurs as the canvas is worked. The primary cause of distortion is the stitches themselves, with the diagonal and crossing stitches generally distorting the work more than straight stitches. Stitch distortion can be compounded by using too tight a stitch tension or too thick a wool for the canvas gauge; it can be minimised by working the canvas on a frame. There are three methods of blocking; which one you use will depend on how misshapen your canvas is. Before blocking, check for any missed stitches.

Use Method 1, below, for canvases with little or no distortion. For these, all that is needed is a light steam-pressing to straighten up the shape and even out the stitch surface. Method 2, top right, is

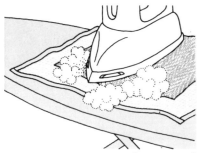

Method 1. Lightly steam-press the canvas work from the wrong side; let it dry thoroughly.

for canvases that show noticeable distortion; Method 3, on the immediate right, is for those that are extremely distorted. With either of these last two methods, the canvas is stretched to match the pattern made of it before it was worked (p. 58). With any method, it is important to let the canvas dry thoroughly before it is moved. If it is still out of shape after drying is complete, block it again.

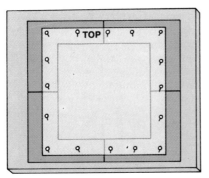

Method 2: 1. Place pattern of prepared canvas right side up on blocking board; cover it with a sheet of tissue paper. Pin both to board.

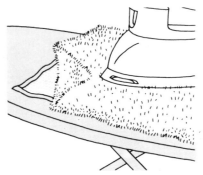

2. Place canvas work face down on ironing board. Dampen a towel and use it to steam-press and dampen the canvas work.

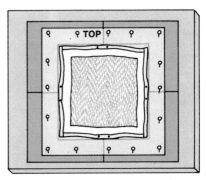

3. Place canvas work face upwards on the pattern and stretch so that its centres and edges match those on pattern. Pin every 2 cm; let dry.

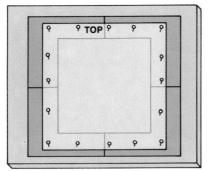

Method 3: 1. Place pattern of prepared canvas right side up on blocking board; cover it with a sheet of tissue paper. Pin both to board.

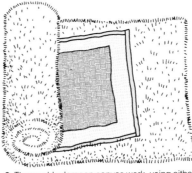

2. Thoroughly dampen canvas work, using either of the following methods. Roll canvas work in a damp towel and leave it rolled until moisture has penetrated both the stitches and the canvas (above left); or sprinkle or sponge the canvas work with enough warm water to dampen it (above right).

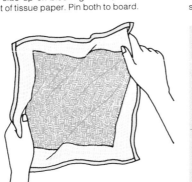

3. Stretch canvas in the direction opposite to the distortion. Begin by pulling at opposite corners; then pull along opposite edges.

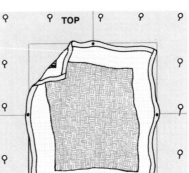

4. Place the canvas work face upwards on the pattern. Stretch canvas so that the centre markings at its edges match those on pattern. Pin.

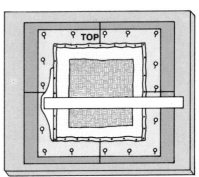

5. Stretch canvas to align its edges with those on pattern; pin in place every 2 cm. Use a T-square to check straightness of canvas threads.

Index